THE BOOK OF
North African
COOKING

THE BOOK OF
North African
COOKING

LESLEY MACKLEY

PHOTOGRAPHED BY
SIMON BUTCHER

PUBLISHED BY
SALAMANDER BOOKS LIMITED
LONDON

Published by Salamander Books Limited
8 Blenheim Court, Brewery Road, London N7 9NT

9 8 7 6 5 4 3 2 1

© Salamander Books Ltd., 1998

ISBN 0 84065 015 X

Produced by: ZEBU Design
Project co-ordinator: Vicky Zentner
Editor: Madeline Weston
Art Director: Vicky Zentner
Photographer: Simon Butcher
Photographer's Assistant: Giles Stokoe
Home Economist: Nicola Fowler
Home Economist's Assistant: Kate Jay
Stylist: Shannon Beare
Filmset by: SX DTP Ltd, Essex
Colour Separations: Emirates Printing Press, Dubai
Printed in Spain by Bookprint, S.L.

Notes
All spoon measurements are level
1 teaspoon = 5ml spoon
1 tablespoon = 15ml spoon

CONTENTS

FOREWORD

The appearance of couscous and harissa on our supermarket shelves, and tagines and couscoussières in cookshops and hardware stores, is a sure sign that our passion for Mediterranean food has now extended to the shores of North Africa. An abundance of fine ingredients, the influence of the various civilisations who have passed through or settled in the area, and the innate hospitality and generosity of the North African people all combine to make this one of the most varied and interesting cuisines in the world. Fragrant stews of meltingly tender meat and dried fruits, hot and spicy marinated and grilled fish, saffron-scented couscous and rice, colourful salads and desserts of sun-ripened fruits and nuts cannot fail to tempt and delight.

With over 80 beautifully illustrated recipes, this book brings you the range and variety of North African cooking. Classic dishes such as Tunisian Brik with Tuna, Chicken Tagine, Moroccan Couscous, Bistilla and Marrakesh Serpent Cake are found alongside new ways with traditional ingredients such as Lamb with Chick-pea Mash and Goats' Cheese and Fig Dressing. There are dishes for every occasion and many are suitable for vegetarians, but whatever your taste, all the recipes will bring the colour and flavour of North Africa to your table.

NORTH AFRICAN COOKING

The North African countries of Morocco, Algeria, Tunisia and Egypt have much in common in their styles of cooking. They share similarities of climate and landscape, but more importantly, a combination of different influences from the cultures of the ancient civilisations that invaded and traded along the southern shores of the Mediterranean Sea. North African cooking is a happy marriage of the cooking styles of the ancient Mediterranean, the Near East and Persia, whose influence is seen in the mixing of ingredients and spices. In addition, many ideas are borrowed and adapted from France and Italy and there is much evidence of Moorish history. Although in many kitchens the mortar and pestle has now given way to the food processor, most North African cooks are determined to pass their traditions on to future generations. Recipes have been handed down through the centuries and adapted to reflect regional and seasonal availability. As with all the Mediterranean countries, the North African diet is extremely healthy, with abundant fresh fruit, vegetables, salads, pulses, bread, herbs, olive oil, fish and grilled meat.

THE NORTH AFRICAN MEAL

Arabs are extremely hospitable and entertain warmly. Meals are expanded to accommodate unexpected guests and any visitor to the house is offered food and drink. Much of the cooking is done in company, with mothers, sisters and daughters all sharing in the food preparation. Although modern kitchens usually contain a gas or electric cooker, many cooks still prefer to cook outdoors on a charcoal brazier. Meals are leisurely and sociable and take place at low round tables. Food is eaten with two fingers and the thumb of the right hand and at a traditional meal each person dips into the same serving dish. A large variety of mezze is served before a meal, or to accompany drinks at any time. There may be anything from four to forty different dishes and can be as simple as nuts, cheese or pickles or miniature versions of main meal dishes.

Soups tend not to be served as a first course, but as a meal in themselves. They are often very substantial and are served with bread. Soup is sold in the streets early in the morning as breakfast for people on their way to work. A bowl of soup, especially harira, is the usual way to end the days of fasting during Ramadan.

A main dish could be a slowly simmered stew of meat or poultry with vegetables or grilled fish or meat. Salads and cold vegetables are present at most meals and couscous or rice and bread will also be served. For a special occasion a whole lamb might be spit-roasted over a fire, and the traditional couscous stew is usually served as a party dish.

Desserts, other than a bowl of fruit, are not normally eaten at everyday meals, but are saved for visitors and festive occasions, when sweet pastries, stuffed with nuts and bathed in syrup, are very popular.

Sweet mint tea is served at the end of a meal to aid digestion. It is served in brass pots and is poured through the long narrow spout into tea glasses. The serving and drinking of coffee is surrounded by tradition and is a very important activity. Men gather in cafés to drink strong coffee, often flavoured with cardamom, in tiny cups, and any visitor is always greeted with freshly made coffee, brewed in long handled copper or brass pots called ibriks.

Sweet syrupy drinks and sherbets are very popular and are widely sold on the streets. Alcohol is prohibited by Muslim dietary laws, but as a legacy from years of French occupation, Morocco has the best wine industry in North Africa and wine drinking nowadays is quite widespread. Thibarine and boukha are favourite liqueurs made from figs.

MEAT

Meat has always been a comparative luxury in North Africa, so it is not served at every meal and is often 'stretched' by combining with vegetables. Traditionally, mutton and lamb are the most widely used meats, but beef and veal are becoming popular. Lamb is prepared in a variety of ways. Legs and shoulders are roasted for special occasions, cubes of lamb are grilled on skewers and less tender cuts

of lamb and beef are marinated and cooked slowly. Minced lamb or beef is popular as a filling for savoury pastries and for stuffing vegetables.

POULTRY AND GAME
A whole roasted chicken is a usual festive dish, and chicken pieces are frequently cooked in casseroles. Lean chicken breast meat is ideal for marinating to keep it moist, then grilling. Pheasant, duck, goose, quail and pigeon are frequently eaten and turkey is becoming more popular.

DAIRY PRODUCE
Traditionally, sheep and goats have been the main dairy animals of North Africa, but cows' milk is now produced throughout the area. Processed yogurt, cheese and samn (a strongly flavoured ghee-type butter) are often eaten. Milk products and eggs form an essential part of breakfast, which will include yogurt and cheese, especially a salt preserved white cheese. Eggs are popular and are served hard-boiled, stuffed, fried, scrambled or in omelettes. Hard-boiled eggs are often used to decorate stews, and are dyed for festive occasions.

FISH AND SHELLFISH
The waters of the North African coast are home to a wide range of fish and shellfish. Morocco is bordered by the Atlantic and the Mediterranean, providing fish from two different seas. Whole fried or grilled fish is particularly popular but there are also many recipes for stews and soups. Red and grey mullet are widely used, as are turbot, bass, sea bream, swordfish, tuna, sardines, monkfish as well as shellfish such as scallops, crabs, mussels, prawns and lobster. Squid, cuttlefish and octopus are frequently fried, grilled and stewed.

VEGETABLES
Vegetables are treated with great respect and frequently feature as a dish in their own right rather than as an accompaniment, either stuffed or combined with other substantial ingredients. Courgettes (zucchini), aubergines (eggplants), peppers (capsicums), cucumbers, tomatoes, onions, garlic, lettuce, artichokes, okra or bamia, small tender leaved spinach, beans, leeks and fennel all grow abundantly and are widely used in North African cooking.

FRUIT AND NUTS

A visit to any market will reveal the variety of brightly coloured fruits which flourish in the area. Bananas, peaches, oranges, lemons, mangoes, melons, figs, watermelon, pomegranates, dates, grapes and apricots are all plentiful. Many fruits are dried and used in both sweet and savoury dishes. Orange juice is used to flavour soups, sauces, cakes and pastries and lemon and lime juice is squeezed onto meat, fish or poultry before grilling.

Preserved lemons add a distinctive flavour to many dishes, and they are easy to make. You need 6 unwaxed, thin-skinned lemons. Scrub them well and soak in cold water for 2 days, changing the water once. Quarter the lemons from the top to within 1cm (½in) of the bottom. Measure 115g (4oz) coarse salt and sprinkle some salt into the cut flesh and reshape the lemons. Place half the remaining salt in the bottom of a preserving jar, then pack in the lemons. Add the remaining salt and press down on the lemons. Cover with freshly squeezed lemon juice and seal the jars. Keep for at least one month. Rinse thoroughly before using in recipes.

Olives and vines are also very important crops. Olives are served at nearly every meal and olive oil is an essential oil for frying, marinating, dressing and sauces. Grapes are used as dessert grapes and for wine making and the leaves are wrapped around a variety of fillings to make dolmades.

Nuts are grown throughout North Africa and are used in both sweet and savoury dishes. Walnuts and hazelnuts are both popular, but almonds, pistachio nuts and pine nuts are particularly valued.

HERBS, SPICES AND FLAVOURINGS

Herbs and spices are used, not only for their taste, but also for their medicinal and therapeutic value. A bunch of herbs is often placed on the dining table for guests to help themselves during the meal. The favourite herbs in North African cooking are flat leaved parsley and mint, but oregano, wild marjoram, thyme, coriander and basil also feature heavily. Dried mint has a more concentrated flavour than the fresh herb and is often used in preference to fresh.

Every town has a spice street in the souk or market and spices have an important place in North African cooking. The most widely used are cinnamon, cumin, coriander, saffron, turmeric, ginger, black pepper, cayenne, paprika, allspice, aniseed, sesame seeds, caraway and cloves. **Tahini** is an oily paste made from crushed sesame seeds and is used in sauces and dips. **Ground sumac** is a less widely known spice which is used to add a sour flavour in marinades and salad dressings, or is rubbed onto meat, fish or chicken before grilling.

There are several spice blends which are essential to North African cooking. **Harissa** is a fiery chilli sauce which is used as a table condiment and is stirred into soups and stews or added to the sauce for couscous. Every spice merchant has his own recipe of **Ras el Hanout**, which can contain as many as 20 different spices. The mixture is sold whole, then ground by the cook as required. **La Kama** is another simpler blend that contains only five spices – cinnamon, black peppercorns, ginger, turmeric and nutmeg. Used to flavour soups and stews, it is especially good with lamb. **Tabil** is specific to Tunisia. It literally means coriander, but usually refers to a blend of coriander seeds, caraway seeds, garlic and dried crushed chilli. The ingredients are pounded together then dried before grinding. **Zahtar** is a mixture of ground sumac and powdered dried thyme combined with an equal quantity of toasted sesame seeds.

Other popular flavourings include rosewater and orange flower water, which only need to be used in small amounts to add fragrance and flavour to many sweet dishes. Pomegranates are used for flavouring in several different ways. The dried seeds have an astringent aroma and sweet-sour taste. They are often crushed and sprinkled on hummus, or added to fruit salads. Pomegranate syrup is frequently used and has an intense flavour.

PULSES AND GRAINS

Traditionally, pulses were dried for use during the winter months and they still feature very strongly in a wide variety of North African dishes, especially salads, soups, stews and bean purées or dips. All kinds of lentils are popular and chick-peas and beans, particularly broad beans, appear at most meals. Dried broad beans are particularly popular in Egypt where they are used to make the classic 'ful medames'.

Wheat is an important crop, and the variety grown in this area is a hard durum wheat, which is ideal for making bread. A wide range of leavened and unleavened bread is produced and is eaten with every meal, often being used as a scoop to pick up food. Many people still make their own bread, frequently cooking on an open fire or in a charcoal oven.

Wheat flour is also used for making the pastry which is used in the many sweet and savoury pastry parcels; these come in a wide variety of shapes – squares, triangles, cylinders and semi-circles. Each country has its own variation on filo pastry. The warka pastry of Morocco is rarely made at home as it requires a high level of skill and is very time consuming. Tunisia's malsouqua pastry is made into pastries known as briks.

Wheat also provides the semolina for making couscous. Nowadays, much of the couscous sold is 'instant' which is pre-prepared and only needs soaking briefly before steaming for a few minutes to warm it through. It is generally felt that the traditional couscous that requires more lengthy preparation is superior in texture and flavour. Unless stated otherwise, the recipes in this book use the instant variety, but if time allows, the regular couscous could be used instead.

Bulgar wheat is made of boiled grains of cracked wheat. It has a light nutty taste and can be used in similar ways to couscous. Secondary cereal crops include rice and maize.

EQUIPMENT

North African kitchens tend to be basic and cooking utensils and equipment are limited; a reflection of the elegant simplicity of most North African cooking. Ovens have only recently been introduced to domestic kitchens and it is more usual for dishes to be simmered on top of the heat than in the oven. The source of heat is often a charcoal brazier or mishmir, and if a dish requires a browned top an earthenware platter heaped with burning charcoal will be placed on it.

Essential pieces of equipment include a couscoussière for cooking meat, fish, poultry and vegetables. They are made of tin, aluminium, copper, stainless steel or even earthenware and consist of a bellied pot or gdra at the base with a steamer or kskas to fit on top. The steamer's perforated base allows the steam from whatever is cooking below to penetrate the couscous in the top. A muslin lined colander on top of a stock pot can be used as a substitute.

Most kitchens will contain several tagines – the glazed earthenware dishes with a conical earthenware cover. They are used for cooking stews of meat, poultry, fish or vegetables. Only a small amount of liquid is added to these dishes and the shape of the lid allows the steam in the dish to condense back into the food so that it does not dry out. Tagines are designed for use on a charcoal cooker and if they are used on gas or electric hotplates they must be placed on a heat diffuser. A tagine with a cast iron base that can be used on any type of stove is now available. The shallow base enables diners to help themselves. A conventional casserole can be used instead of a tagine but the food will have to be transferred to platters if you wish to eat with your fingers in the traditional manner.

Other pieces of equipment found in most kitchens include a gsaa or large round earthenware basin used for kneading bread dough and a midouna, which is a large flat basket used for separating the grains of couscous. There will also be a collection of skewers, sometimes in silver, for cooking brochettes, and there may be a damossa, which is a wide bellied pot with a slender neck for cooking over an outdoor fire. Most of the other cooking pots in the kitchen will be earthenware or tin-lined copper. There will also be copper, silver and brass serving trays, teapots, tea glasses and coffee pots.

HARIRA

4 tablespoons olive oil
1 large onion, finely chopped
2 cloves garlic, crushed
1 teaspoon turmeric
1 teaspoon ground ginger
1 teaspoon ground cumin
1.5 litres (53 fl oz) chicken or vegetable stock
225 g (8 oz/1¼ cups) green lentils, washed
400 g (14 oz) can chopped tomatoes
400 g (14 oz) can chick-peas, drained
3 tablespoons chopped fresh coriander
3 tablespoons chopped fresh parsley
salt and freshly ground black pepper
lemon juice, optional
olive oil and harissa (see page 46), to serve

In a large saucepan, heat half the oil. Add the onion and cook for 10 minutes, until soft. Add the garlic, turmeric, ginger and cumin and cook for a few more minutes. Stir in the stock and add the lentils and tomatoes. Bring to the boil, cover and simmer for 20 minutes or until the lentils are soft. Stir in the chick-peas, remaining olive oil, coriander, parsley, salt, pepper and lemon juice, if using, and simmer for 5 more minutes.

To serve, pour some olive oil into a small bowl and spoon some harissa into another small bowl. Ladle the soup into heated bowls and place the olive oil and harissa on the table for people to help themselves.

Serves 6-8.

Note: 115 g (4 oz) dried chick-peas may be used instead of canned ones. They should be soaked overnight and simmered for 1 hour or until soft, before adding with the lentils.

SPINACH SOUP

250 g (9 oz) young fresh spinach
115 g (4 oz/¼ cup) long grain rice
2 tablespoons olive oil
1 onion, finely chopped
2 cloves garlic, crushed
1 teaspoon ground coriander
4 spring onions (scallions), finely chopped
1 litre (35 fl oz/4½ cups) vegetable or chicken stock
salt and freshly ground black pepper
500 ml (18 fl oz/2¼ cups) Greek yogurt
grated lemon rind, to garnish

Remove any coarse stalks from the spinach. Wash the spinach in plenty of water and drain thoroughly. Cut into shreds.

Wash the rice in several changes of water and leave to drain. In a large saucepan, heat the oil. Add the onion and garlic and cook for 10 minutes, until soft. Stir in the ground coriander and cook for 2 more minutes. Stir in the spring onions (scallions) and the drained rice. Pour in the stock and season with salt and pepper.

Bring to the boil, cover and simmer gently for 10 minutes then add the spinach and cook for 5 minutes until the rice and spinach are cooked. The rice should not be too soft. Stir the yogurt into the soup. Heat without boiling and pour into warmed bowls. Serve, garnished with lemon rind.

Serves 6.

—SQUASH SOUP & MINT PURÉE—

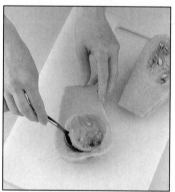

1 butternut squash, about 450g (1lb)
25 g (1 oz) butter
1 onion, finely chopped
1 clove garlic, crushed
½ teaspoon each ground turmeric and ground cumin
850 ml (30 fl oz/3¾ cups) chicken or vegetable stock
salt and freshly ground black pepper
toasted cumin seeds, to garnish
MINT PURÉE
1 small bunch fresh mint
2 tablespoons olive oil
1 teaspoon lemon juice

Peel the squash, remove the seeds and roughly chop the flesh.

In a large saucepan, heat the butter. Add the chopped onion and cook gently for 10 minutes until soft. Stir in the garlic, turmeric and cumin and cook, stirring, for 2 more minutes. Add the pieces of squash and stock and season with salt and pepper. Bring to the boil then cover and simmer for 20 minutes until the squash is soft.

Meanwhile, make the mint purée. In a mortar and pestle, pound the mint with a large pinch of salt. Add the olive oil and lemon juice and mix to a purée. In a blender or food processor, process the squash soup until smooth. Check the seasoning and pour into heated bowls. Add a spoonful of purée to each and garnish with toasted cumin seeds.

Serves 4-6.

Note: If butternut squash is not available, other squashes such as pumpkin may be used.

SEAFOOD SOUP

450g (1 lb) firm fish fillets
450g (1 lb) mixed prepared raw shellfish, such as
  prawns in the shell, squid, scallops
1 quantity chermoula (see page 42)
1 red pepper (capsicum), seeded and chopped
a few mussels
chopped fresh parsley, to serve
FISH STOCK
fish trimmings such as bones, heads, prawn shells etc.
2 onions, sliced
70ml (2½fl oz/⅓ cup) olive oil
8 black peppercorns
handful mixed coriander and parsley, including stalks
3 cloves garlic, sliced
4 tomatoes, roughly chopped
salt

To make the stock, in a saucepan put the fish
trimmings, onions, olive oil, peppercorns,
coriander, parsley, garlic, tomatoes and salt.
Add 2 litres (2¼ pints/9 cups) water and
bring to the boil. Simmer gently, uncovered,
for 45 minutes. Press the stock through a
sieve into a clean pan. Cut the fish into
cubes and place in a bowl with the shellfish.
Add half the chermoula. Mix well to coat
thoroughly, then cover the bowl and refrigerate for 30 minutes.

Add the red pepper (capsicum) to the fish
stock and simmer for 5 minutes until the
pepper is tender. Add the fish and shellfish
and simmer for 3-4 minutes until the fish is
cooked. Add the mussels and cook for
2 more minutes or until they open. Discard
any mussels that do not open. Adjust the
seasoning and spoon into heated bowls.
Serve with a little of the remaining chermoula in each bowl. Scatter the parsley over.

Serves 6 as a main meal or 8 as a first course.

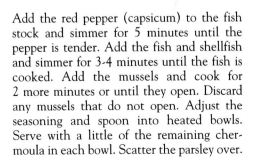

—LENTIL SOUP WITH ROCKET—

2 tablespoons olive oil
1 onion, finely chopped
2 cloves garlic, crushed
1 teaspoon ground cumin
1.5 litres (53 fl oz) chicken or vegetable stock
200 g (7 oz/1 cup) red lentils
225 g (8 oz) rocket (arugula)
salt and freshly ground black pepper
olive oil, to serve

In a large saucepan, heat the olive oil. Add the onion and garlic and cook for 10 minutes until soft.

Stir in the cumin and cook for 2 more minutes. Add the stock and bring to the boil then stir in the lentils. Cover and simmer for 20 minutes or until the lentils are soft, but not disintegrating.

Chop the rocket (arugula), including the stalks, very roughly and add to the soup. Season with salt and pepper, cover and simmer for 2 more minutes. To serve, pour the soup into heated soup bowls and drizzle a little olive oil over.

Serves 6.

—CUCUMBER & YOGURT SOUP—

1 large cucumber
550 ml (20 fl oz/2½ cups) Greek yogurt
2 cloves garlic, crushed
finely grated rind of 1 lemon
2 tablespoons chopped fresh mint
salt and freshly ground black pepper
mint leaves, to garnish

Rinse the cucumber and trim the ends. Do not peel. Grate the cucumber into a bowl.

Stir in the yogurt, garlic, lemon rind and chopped mint. Season well with salt and pepper. Cover the bowl and chill for 1 hour.

Stir in 150 ml (5 fl oz/⅔ cup) iced water. Add more water if the soup seems a little thick. Adjust the seasoning then pour into chilled soup bowls. Garnish with mint leaves.

Serves 6.

Variation: Cooked, peeled prawns may be added to this soup.

BABA GANOUSH

2 small aubergines (eggplants)
1 clove garlic, crushed
4 tablespoons tahini
25 g (1 oz/¼ cup) ground almonds
juice of ½ lemon
½ teaspoon ground cumin
salt and freshly ground black pepper
1 tablespoon chopped fresh mint leaves
2 tablespoons olive oil
fresh mint leaves, to garnish
selection of vegetables such as baby artichokes,
 radishes, sliced peppers (capsicums), to serve

Place aubergines (eggplants) under a hot grill, turning often, until black and blistered.

Remove the skins, chop the flesh roughly and leave to drain in a colander for 10 minutes. Squeeze out as much liquid from the aubergines (eggplants) as possible and place the flesh in a food processor or blender. Add garlic, tahini, ground almonds, lemon juice, cumin, salt and pepper and process to a smooth paste.

Stir the chopped mint leaves into the dip. Spoon into a bowl and drizzle with olive oil. Scatter mint leaves on top. Place the bowl on a serving platter and serve with the vegetable selection.

Serves 6.

BISSARA

450g (1 lb) frozen broad beans
4 cloves garlic, crushed
3 spring onions (scallions), roughly chopped
1 teaspoon ground cumin
2 tablespoons each chopped fresh mint, chopped
  fresh coriander, and chopped fresh parsley
salt
pinch cayenne pepper
juice of ½ lemon
toasted Arab bread, olive oil and cayenne pepper, to
  serve

Boil the beans for 5 minutes, or until tender. Drain, reserving a little of the cooking liquid, and refresh in cold water. Drain again.

Slip the beans out of their skins and place in a food processor or blender with the garlic. Process to a rough purée then add the spring onions (scallions), cumin, mint, coriander, parsley, salt, cayenne pepper and lemon juice. Process again until thoroughly blended. Add enough of the reserved cooking liquid to make a spreading consistency.

To serve, spread the purée on the toasted bread. Drizzle a little olive oil over and sprinkle with cayenne pepper. Cut into smaller pieces, as desired.

Serves 6-8.

Note: Bissara is traditionally made with dried broad beans.

Variation: Add sufficient cooking liquid to make a dipping consistency and serve with raw vegetables.

—CARROT SALAD WITH PITTA—

450g (1 lb) carrots, peeled and thickly sliced
2 cloves garlic, crushed
¼ teaspoon cayenne pepper
½ teaspoon ground cumin
½ teaspoon ground allspice
½ teaspoon sugar
juice of ½ lemon
salt and freshly ground black pepper
200ml (7 fl oz) olive oil
4 pitta breads
fresh mint leaves, to garnish
ZAHTAR
55g (2 oz) sesame seeds
25g (1 oz) ground sumac
25g (1 oz) ground dried thyme

Boil carrots for 5-10 minutes until soft. Drain, refresh in cold water and drain again. Place in a food processor or blender with garlic, cayenne pepper, cumin, allspice, sugar, lemon juice, salt and pepper. Process until smooth; continue to process while trickling in 4 tablespoons of the olive oil. Check seasoning and transfer to a serving bowl. Cover and chill for 2 hours. To make the zahtar, in a heavy frying pan (skillet), dry roast sesame seeds over a medium heat, stirring, until lightly browned. Place in a bowl and leave to cool. Stir in sumac and thyme. Set aside.

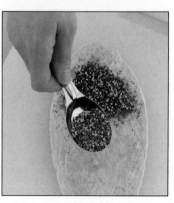

Split the pitta breads in half. Drizzle the remaining olive oil over the cut sides of the bread and sprinkle 1 tablespoon of zahtar over each piece. Grill under a warm grill until browned and crisp. When cool, break into rough pieces. Allow the carrot salad to come to room temperature. Garnish with mint leaves and serve with the pitta toasts.

Serves 6.

Note: Store the unused zahtar in a screw-top jar for up to 3 months.

DUKKAH

115 g (4 oz) sesame seeds
45 g (2 oz) shelled, skinned hazelnuts
45 g (2 oz) coriander seeds
25 g (1 oz) ground cumin
1 teaspoon dried thyme
1 teaspoon salt
½ teaspoon freshly ground black pepper
bread and olive oil, to serve

Heat a large heavy frying pan (skillet) over a medium heat. Add the sesame seeds and roast, stirring, until they are a light golden brown. Set aside to cool.

Add the hazelnuts to the pan and roast, stirring until lightly and evenly browned. Set aside to cool. Add the coriander seeds to the pan and roast until they begin to pop. Set aside to cool. Place the sesame seeds, hazelnuts, coriander seeds, cumin, thyme, salt and pepper in a food processor or blender and process to a coarse powder.

Transfer the dukkah to a serving bowl. To serve, dip a piece of bread into the olive oil and then into the dukkah mixture.

Serves 6.

Note: Take care not to over-grind the nuts and seeds otherwise they will release their oils and form a paste. Dukkah can be made in large quantities and stored in an airtight container.

—MARINATED OLIVES—

115g (4oz/¾ cup) black olives
115g (4oz/¾ cup) green olives
1 preserved lemon (see page 10)
1 tablespoon coriander seeds
2 cloves garlic
3 dried red chillies
2 bay leaves
1 teaspoon green peppercorns in brine, drained
olive oil

Make 2 or 3 cuts lengthways in each olive. Place them in a bowl. Cut the peel from the preserved lemon into small pieces and add to the olives.

In a mortar and pestle, lightly crush the coriander seeds and add to the olives. Crush the garlic and add to the olives with the dried chillies, bay leaves and green peppercorns. Mix well.

Spoon the olives into a preserving jar or screw-top jar. Cover with olive oil and seal the jar tightly. Leave to marinate in a cool dry place for 1 week, turning the jar occasionally. To serve, transfer to a serving bowl and serve as an appetizer with drinks or as part of a selection of mezzes.

Serves 6.

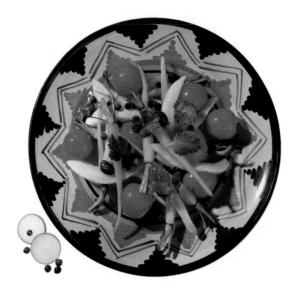

PICKLED VEGETABLES

225 g (8 oz) baby carrots
225 g (8 oz) radishes, trimmed
1 fennel bulb, sliced
2 teaspoons salt
4 tablespoons white wine vinegar
4 tablespoons sugar
1 tablespoon green peppercorns in brine, drained
1 tablespoon capers
freshly ground black pepper
coriander leaves, to garnish

Peel and trim the carrots, leaving some green leaves attached at the top. Place in a bowl.

Add the radishes and fennel slices to the carrots in the bowl. Sprinkle the salt over and leave for 2 hours. Drain the vegetables and rinse with cold water. Pat dry and return to the bowl.

In a saucepan, heat the vinegar and sugar, without boiling, until the sugar is dissolved. Pour the vinegar mixture over the vegetables and add the peppercorns, capers and pepper. Leave until cold then cover and refrigerate overnight. Serve the vegetables garnished with coriander leaves.

Serves 6.

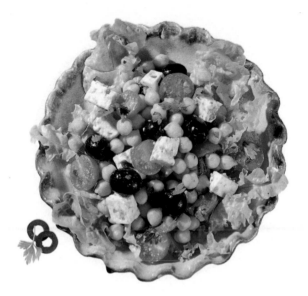

–CHICK-PEA, FETA & OLIVE SALAD–

2 x 400g (14oz) cans chick-peas, drained and rinsed
150g (5oz) feta cheese, cut into cubes
225g (8oz) cherry tomatoes
55g (2oz) pitted black olives
4 tablespoons flat leaf parsley
salad leaves, to serve
HARISSA DRESSING
70ml (2½ fl oz) olive oil
1 tablespoon lemon juice
1 clove garlic, crushed
2 teaspoons harissa (see page 46)
salt

Place the chick-peas in a bowl and add the
feta cheese cubes.

Unless the cherry tomatoes are very small,
cut them in half and add to the chick-peas
and feta cheese. Add the black olives and
the flat leaf parsley.

To make the dressing, in a bowl whisk
together the olive oil, lemon juice, garlic,
harissa and salt. Pour the dressing over the
chick-pea and tomato mixture and mix
gently together. Arrange the salad leaves on
six plates and pile the salad on top. Serve
immediately.

Serves 6.

-GOATS' CHEESE & FIG DRESSING-

55g (2oz/⅓ cup) couscous
45g (1½oz) pine nuts, finely chopped
salt and freshly ground black pepper
1 tablespoon plain flour
1 egg, beaten
2 x 100g (3½oz) soft goats' cheeses, cut in half
   horizontally
vegetable oil for frying
salad leaves, to serve
FIG DRESSING
6 tablespoons olive oil
3 tablespoons lemon juice
3 tablespoons orange juice
1 teaspoon cumin seeds, roughly crushed
2 teaspoons pink peppercorns, roughly crushed
2 ripe figs

Place the couscous in a bowl and just cover with boiling water. Leave to soak for a few minutes. Fluff up the grains with a fork, then spread out on a baking sheet to dry for about 20 minutes. The grains should not dry completely. Place in a bowl, stir in the pine nuts and season with salt and pepper. Sift the flour onto a plate and pour the beaten egg into a shallow dish. Roll each cheese slice in the flour, then dip into the egg. Roll in the couscous to coat completely. Wrap each coated slice in cling film and chill for 1 hour.

To make the fig dressing, in a bowl, whisk together olive oil, lemon juice, orange juice, cumin seeds, pink peppercorns, salt and black pepper. Trim the fig stalks and cut the flesh into tiny dice. Stir into the vinaigrette and set aside. Arrange salad leaves on 4 plates. In a frying pan (skillet), heat about 1cm (½in) oil. Add the cheese slices to the pan and fry, turning once, until the crust is lightly browned. Place a slice on each plated, drizzle with the dressing, and serve.

Serves 4.

— SESAME-HERB LABNA BALLS —

500 ml (18 fl oz/2¼ cups) live cows' or goats' milk
  yogurt
a little cream or crème fraîche, optional
1 teaspoon salt
2 tablespoons sesame seeds
1 tablespoon chopped fresh parsley
1 tablespoon chopped fresh mint
vine leaves, to decorate

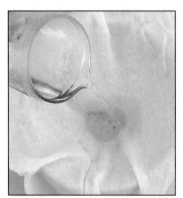

Place a non-reactive colander or sieve over a bowl. Place a large double square of muslin in the colander and pour boiling water through, to scald it. Pour off the water.

Pour the yogurt into the muslin square. Add the cream or crème fraîche, if using. Draw up the sides and corners of the muslin and tie with string. Hang the muslin bag over the bowl and leave in a cool place overnight. Tip the curds into a bowl and stir in the salt. Replace in the muslin and hang over the bowl again for several more hours. Roll the cheese into balls and chill for 1 hour.

Heat a frying pan (skillet) and add the sesame seeds. Heat until golden brown, stirring frequently. Transfer to a plate and leave to cool. On a plate, mix together the chopped parsley and mint. Roll half the balls in the sesame seeds and half in the herbs. Decorate with vine leaves and serve with pitta bread.

Serves 4.

Variation: Instead of rolling the mixture into balls, serve with olive oil drizzled over.

STUFFED ONION PETALS

1 large mild onion, peeled and quartered
large pinch saffron threads
salt and freshly ground black pepper
1 tablespoon olive oil
2 cloves garlic, crushed
1 teaspoon cumin seeds
225 g (8 oz) peeled cooked new potatoes
2 tablespoons pine nuts
4 tablespoons Greek yogurt
1 tablespoon chopped fresh coriander
fresh coriander leaves, to garnish

Separate the layers of the onion quarters to make 'petals', reserving the central core.

Add the saffron and onion petals to a large pan of boiling salted water. Boil for 15 minutes, making sure they do not clump together, until thoroughly cooked and soft. Drain and dry on kitchen paper. Leave to cool. Finely chop the reserved onion core. Heat the oil in a frying pan. Add the chopped onion, garlic and cumin seeds and cook gently for 10 minutes or until the onion is soft. Set aside to cool.

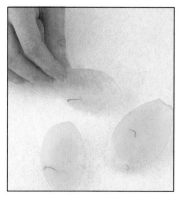

Cut the potatoes into tiny dice, place in a bowl and add the cooled onion mixture, pine nuts, yogurt, chopped coriander, salt and pepper. Mix together gently. Place a teaspoon of the stuffing into each onion petal and gently press up the sides around the filling, forming canoe shapes with pointed ends. Arrange on a serving dish and garnish with coriander leaves.

Serves 4-6.

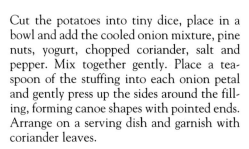

AUBERGINE STACKS

70 ml (2½fl oz) olive oil
1 onion, finely chopped
1 clove garlic, crushed
1 red pepper (capsicum), seeded and chopped
400 g (14 oz) can chopped tomatoes
25 g (1 oz) sun-dried tomatoes in oil, drained and
  chopped
1 tablespoon raisins
½ teaspoon sugar
2 teaspoons balsamic vinegar
salt and freshly ground black pepper
1 teaspoon dried mint
4 medium long-shaped aubergines (eggplants)
fresh mint sprigs, to garnish

In a saucepan, heat 2 tablespoons of the olive oil. Add the onion and garlic and cook for 10 minutes or until soft. Add the pepper (capsicum), canned tomatoes, sun-dried tomatoes, raisins, sugar, vinegar, salt, pepper and mint. Simmer gently, uncovered, for 20 minutes or until the mixture has thickened. Meanwhile, cut the aubergines (eggplants) into 5 mm (¼in) thick slices. Brush each slice on both sides with remaining olive oil.

Heat a ridged cast iron grill pan and grill the aubergine (eggplant) slices for 3-4 minutes on each side until soft and browned. Keep hot while cooking the remaining slices. Spoon a little of the tomato mixture on an aubergine (eggplant) slice. Top with a second slice. Keep warm. Repeat with the remaining aubergine (eggplant) slices and tomato mixture. Serve garnished with mint sprigs.

Serves 6.

ROAST VEGETABLE CUPS

2 medium aubergines (eggplants), cut into 2 cm
  (¾in) cubes
4 medium courgettes (zucchini), cut into 2 cm (¾in)
  cubes
1 red onion, chopped
2 cloves garlic, crushed
4 tablespoons olive oil
juice of ½ lemon
2 teaspoons dried oregano
salt and freshly ground black pepper
45 g (1½oz) butter, melted
6 sheets filo pastry, 40x30 cm (16x12 in)
strips of sun-dried tomatoes and toasted pine nuts, to
  garnish

Preheat the oven to 200C (400F/Gas 6).
Place the aubergines (eggplants), courgettes
(zucchini) and onion in a large roasting tin.
Add the garlic, olive oil, lemon juice,
oregano, salt and pepper and mix well. Roast
for 30 minutes, stirring occasionally, until
tender and slightly browned. Meanwhile,
prepare the filo cups. Invert 12 individual
ramekins on a baking sheet. Brush lightly
with melted butter. Brush one sheet of pastry
with melted butter and cut into 6 squares.
Press 1 square, butter side up, over an
upturned ramekin.

Repeat with a second square at an angle so
that the points form petals. Repeat with a
third square. Cover remaining ramekins in
the same way. Remove vegetables from oven
and keep warm. Reduce oven temperature to
190C (375F/Gas 5). Bake the cups for
10 minutes until crisp and golden. Ease off
the ramekins and place on a serving dish.
Divide roasted vegetables between the cups.
Garnish with sun-dried tomatoes and pine
nuts and serve with salad.

Makes 12.

—TUNISIAN BRIK WITH TUNA—

1 tablespoon butter
1 small onion, finely chopped
1 clove garlic, crushed
100g (3½oz) can tuna in oil, drained
2 tablespoons chopped fresh parsley
salt and freshly ground black pepper
2 sheets filo pastry, 40x30cm (16x12in)
6 quails' eggs
1 egg white, lightly beaten
vegetable oil for frying
lemon wedges, to garnish

Heat the butter in a frying pan (skillet). Cook the onion and garlic gently for 10 minutes, until soft. Transfer to a bowl; cool.

Add the tuna, parsley, salt and pepper to the onion and mix well. Place one filo sheet on top of the other and cut into 6 squares. Place a spoonful of the tuna mixture on one triangular half of each filo square. Make a slight indentation in the mixture and carefully break a quail's egg into the hollow. Brush the edges of the pastry with beaten egg white and fold to make a triangle. Brush the joined edges again with egg white and fold over a small margin to make a stronger rim. Make 5 more triangular parcels or briks.

Heat 2.5cm (1in) of oil in a large deep frying pan (skillet). The oil should be hot, but not smoking. Slide the briks, in batches, into the hot oil. Spoon oil over the the top while frying. When the underside is lightly browned and crisp, turn and continue frying until the other side is brown. Drain on kitchen paper and keep warm while frying the remaining briks. Garnish with lemon wedges and serve hot, with salad leaves.

Serves 6.

- CHICK·PEA & CORIANDER CAKES -

2 x 425g (15oz) cans chick-peas, drained
2 cloves garlic, crushed
1 bunch spring onions (scallions), chopped
2 teaspoons ground cumin
2 teaspoons ground coriander
1 fresh green chilli, cored, seeded and finely chopped
2 tablespoons chopped fresh coriander
1 small egg, beaten
2 tablespoons plain flour, plus extra for dusting
salt and freshly ground black pepper
vegetable oil for shallow frying
fresh coriander, to garnish
CUCUMBER & YOGURT DIP
½ cucumber, peeled, seeded and diced
150ml (5floz/⅔ cup) Greek yogurt
1 clove garlic, crushed

In a blender or food processor, process the chick-peas until smooth. Add the garlic, spring onions (scallions), cumin and ground coriander. Process again until well combined. Spoon the mixture into a bowl and stir in the chilli, fresh coriander, egg and flour. Mix well and season with salt and pepper. If the mixture is very soft add a little more flour. Chill for about 30 minutes to firm the mixture.

To make cucumber and yogurt dip, place cucumber in a colander, sprinkle with 1 teaspoon salt and leave to drain for 30 minutes. Pat dry with kitchen paper and place in a bowl. Stir in the yogurt and garlic and season with pepper. With floured hands, shape the chick-pea mixture into 12 cakes. In a frying pan (skillet), heat the oil and fry the cakes for 2-3 minutes on each side, until crisp and golden. Drain on kitchen paper. Garnish with fresh coriander and serve with the dip.

Serves 4.

COURGETTE PANCAKES

2 courgettes (zucchini), about 450g (1lb) total
  weight
55g (2oz/½ cup) plain flour
3 eggs
1 teaspoon chopped fresh mint
salt and freshly ground black pepper
vegetable oil for shallow frying
mint sprigs, to garnish
RED PEPPER SAUCE
1 tablespoon olive oil
1 small onion, chopped
1 clove garlic, crushed
2 red peppers (capsicums), seeded and chopped
225ml (8floz/1 cup) vegetable stock

To make the sauce, in a saucepan, heat oil,
add onion and garlic and cook until soft.
Add the red peppers (capsicums) and stock
and simmer for 10 minutes or until soft.
Purée the mixture in a blender or food
processor then press through a sieve. Set
aside. Trim the courgettes (zucchini) and
grate coarsely into a bowl. Sift the flour into
a bowl and beat in the eggs to make a
smooth batter. Stir in the mint and season
with salt and pepper. Squeeze out as much
liquid as possible from the grated courgettes
(zucchini) and stir into the batter.

In a large heavy based frying pan (skillet),
heat some oil. Fry tablespoons of mixture, in
batches, for about 4 minutes each side, until
browned and cooked through. Keep warm
while cooking the remainder. Reheat the red
pepper sauce and serve with the courgette
pancakes, garnished with mint.

Serves 6-8.

—LEEK & BROAD BEAN EGGAH—

3 tablespoons olive oil
2 medium leeks, trimmed, washed and thinly sliced
1 clove garlic, crushed
½ teaspoon sugar
juice of ½ lemon
6 eggs
300g (10oz) fresh or frozen broad beans, cooked
CHERRY TOMATO SALSA
1 tablespoon lemon juice
55ml (2fl oz/¼ cup) olive oil
¼ teaspoon cayenne pepper
1 tablespoon chopped fresh chives
salt and freshly ground black pepper
225g (8oz) cherry tomatoes, halved
4 spring onions (scallions), thinly sliced

Make the cherry tomato salsa. In a bowl, mix together the lemon juice, olive oil, cayenne, chives and salt. Add the tomatoes and spring onions (scallions) and mix well. Set the salsa aside. Heat 1 tablespoon of the oil in a frying pan (skillet), add leeks and garlic and cook gently for 10-15 minutes until leeks are soft and lightly coloured. Stir in sugar and lemon juice and cook briskly to evaporate any liquid. In a large bowl, beat eggs lightly and season with salt and pepper. Stir in leeks and broad beans.

Heat remaining oil in a heavy based 22.5cm (9in) frying pan (skillet). Pour in the egg mixture and cook, covered, over a very low heat for about 20 minutes until almost set, and the underside is browned. Place under a medium grill for 1 or 2 minutes to lightly brown and set the top. Cut into wedges and serve with the tomato salsa.

Serves 4.

Note: This is equally good hot or cold, and can be served as a snack or a main course.

—HUMMUS & GRILLED CHICKEN—

2 boneless, skinless chicken breasts
juice of ½ lemon
70 ml (2½ fl oz/⅓ cup) olive oil
salt and freshly ground black pepper
2 teaspoons toasted sesame seeds
1 teaspoon ground cumin
½ teaspoon paprika
8 slices ciabatta-type bread
salad leaves, to garnish
HUMMUS
425 g (15 oz) can chick-peas, drained
4 tablespoons tahini
4 tablespoons Greek yogurt
2 cloves garlic, crushed
1 tablespoons olive oil
juice of 1 lemon

Place chicken breasts in a shallow dish. In a bowl, mix together lemon juice, 2 tablespoons of the olive oil, salt and pepper and pour over chicken. Cover and leave in a cool place for 1 hour. To make the hummus, place chick-peas, tahini, yogurt, garlic, olive oil, lemon juice, salt and pepper in a blender or food processor and process to form a slightly grainy paste.

Grill the chicken breasts under a preheated grill for 15 minutes, turning once, until cooked through. Cut into slices and keep warm. Mix together the sesame seeds, cumin, paprika and salt. Drizzle the bread on both sides with olive oil and toast under the grill. Spread some hummus on each piece of toast, top with chicken slices and sprinkle with sesame seed mixture. Drizzle with remaining olive oil and serve, garnished with salad leaves.

Serves 4-8.

MOROCCAN LAMB ROLLS

1 tablespoon pine nuts
55 ml (2 fl oz/¼ cup) olive oil
1 onion, finely chopped
350 g (12 oz) lean minced lamb
½ teaspoon ground cinnamon
1 tablespoon chopped fresh mint
salt and freshly ground black pepper
6 sheets filo pastry, 40x30 cm (16x12 in)
fresh mint, to garnish
TAHINI & LEMON DIP
2 tablespoons tahini
juice of 1 lemon
2 cloves garlic, crushed

In a frying pan (skillet), heat pine nuts until golden. Remove from the pan and set aside.

In a frying pan (skillet), heat 2 tablespoons of the oil. Add the onion and cook for 10 minutes until soft. Stir in the lamb and cook, stirring, for a few minutes until browned. Add the cinnamon, mint, pine nuts, salt and pepper. Cook for a further 10 minutes then leave to cool. Preheat the oven to 180C (350F/Gas 4). Cut each sheet of filo pastry across into 3 strips. Brush the strips with the remaining oil.

Spread a spoonful of the lamb filling in a line on one end of each filo strip, leaving a small margin on either side. Roll over twice and fold the long sides over the edge, then continue rolling to make a tube. Place the rolls on a baking sheet. Bake in the oven for 20-30 minutes until crisp and golden. Meanwhile, make the tahini and lemon dip. In a bowl, mix together the tahini, lemon juice and garlic. Garnish the lamb rolls with mint and serve with the dip.

Makes 18.

FISH COUSCOUS

1 tablespoon vegetable oil
2 onions, chopped
225g (8oz) baby carrots, trimmed
225g (8oz) baby turnips, quartered
2 sticks celery, cut into chunks
550ml (20floz/2½ cups) fish stock
salt and freshly ground black pepper
½ teaspoon saffron threads
1½ teaspoons tabil (see page 10)
225g (8oz) baby courgettes (zucchini), trimmed
1 bunch spring onions (scallions)
225g (8oz) tomatoes, peeled and quartered
115g (4oz) shelled peas
1kg (2¼lb) skinless cod fillet
450g (1lb/2½ cups) couscous
harissa (see page 46), to serve

In a large saucepan, heat the oil. Add the
onions and cook gently for 10 minutes until
soft. Add the carrots, turnips, celery and
stock. Season generously with salt and pepper and add the saffron and tabil. Bring to
the boil, cover and simmer for 10 minutes.
Add the courgettes (zucchini) and simmer
for 10 minutes then add the spring onions
(scallions), tomatoes and peas.

Cut the fish into large pieces and place on
top of the vegetables. Cover and simmer for
10 minutes until the fish flakes easily when
tested with a knife. Meanwhile, prepare
couscous as directed on the packet. To serve,
pile couscous in a large heated serving dish.
Arrange vegetables over couscous and place
fish on top. Stir harissa, to taste, into broth
and pour as much as desired over the couscous. Serve extra broth and harissa separately.

Serves 6.

—— SARDINES IN VINE LEAVES ——

3 unwaxed thin-skinned lemons, quartered lengthways
3 tablespoons sea salt
2 tablespoons sugar
12 large vine leaves in brine
12 fresh sardines, scaled and gutted
salad leaves, to garnish
STUFFING
4 tablespoons chopped fresh coriander
4 tablespoons chopped fresh parsley
2 cloves garlic, crushed
salt and freshly ground black pepper
55 ml (2 fl oz/¼ cup) olive oil

Preheat oven to 190C (375F/Gas 5). Place lemon quarters in an ovenproof dish with salt and sugar and mix well. Cover with foil. Bake for 1-1½ hours until soft. Leave to cool. Place the vine leaves in a bowl and cover with cold water. Leave to soak for one hour, changing the water twice. Drain and pat dry. Remove the backbone from the sardines by pressing down along the length of the backbone to flatten them. Pull out the backbone and wash and dry the fish.

To make the stuffing, in a bowl, mix together the coriander, parsley, garlic, salt, pepper and olive oil. Stuff the fish with the herb mixture. Roll each fish up in a vine leaf. Place under a preheated grill or on a barbecue and grill for 3-5 minutes on each side until the vine leaves are crisp and the fish flakes easily when tested with a knife. Garnish with salad leaves, and serve with the roasted lemons.

Serves 4-6.

-FISH WITH COUSBAREIA SAUCE-

4 tomatoes
2 tablespoons olive oil
1 onion, chopped
1 clove garlic, crushed
115g (4oz/¾ cup) hazelnuts, finely chopped
55g (2oz) pine nuts
3 tablespoons chopped fresh parsley
salt and freshly ground black pepper
fillets from 4 red mullet, skinned
parsley sprigs, to garnish

Place the tomatoes in a bowl and cover with
boiling water. Leave for 1 minute then drain
and cover with cold water.

Leave for 1 minute then peel the skins off
the tomatoes. Remove the seeds and cut the
flesh into dice. In a large frying pan (skillet),
heat the oil. Add the onion and garlic and
cook for 10-15 minutes until soft. Add the
hazelnuts and pine nuts and fry for 2 more
minutes. Stir in the tomatoes and cook for 3
or 4 minutes until soft. Add 150ml (5floz/
⅔ cup) water to cover, the parsley, salt and
pepper and simmer for 5 minutes.

Place the red mullet fillets in the pan and
spoon some of the sauce over. Cover and
simmer for 10-15 minutes until the fish
flakes easily when tested with a knife. Serve
the fish fillets on heated plates with the
sauce poured round. Garnish with parsley
sprigs, and serve with salad leaves.

Serves 4.

—STUFFED SEA BASS & SALAD—

1 clove garlic, crushed
salt and freshly ground black pepper
1 tablespoon lime juice
1 teaspoon ground cumin
¼ teaspoon chilli powder
1 tablespoon olive oil
1.35 kg (3 lb) sea bass, cleaned and scaled
1 bag prepared salad leaves
STUFFING
large pinch saffron threads
2 tablespoons olive oil
6 spring onions (scallions), chopped
25 g (1 oz/¼ cup) ready-to-eat dried apricots, chopped
25 g (1 oz/½ cup) fresh breadcrumbs
55 g (2 oz/½ cup) chopped walnuts
¼ teaspoon ground cardamom

In a small bowl, mix together the garlic, salt, 2 teaspoons of the lime juice, cumin, chilli powder and 1 tablespoon olive oil. Make several slashes in the skin of the fish and rub the marinade well in. Cover and leave in the refrigerator for 1 hour. To make the stuffing, place the saffron in a small bowl with 1 tablespoon hot water. In a saucepan, heat 2 tablespoons oil. Add spring onions (scallions) and cook for a few minutes until soft. Stir in apricots, breadcrumbs, walnuts, salt, pepper, cardamom and soaked saffron. Cook for 1 minute then leave to cool.

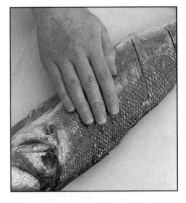

Preheat oven to 180C (350F/Gas 4). Place the fish on a sheet of well oiled foil and fill the cavity with stuffing. Draw foil up to make a parcel. Place on a large baking sheet and bake for 40-50 minutes until fish flakes easily when tested with a knife. To serve, cut into 4 fillets; arrange on 4 heated plates and keep warm. Heat the cooking juices in a pan and add the salad leaves. Stir briefly until just wilted then add remaining lime juice; serve with the fish, and with spicy rice.

Serves 4.

—FISH TAGINE WITH TOMATOES—

8 plum tomatoes, cut in half lengthways
2 teaspoons caster sugar
salt and freshly ground black pepper
2 tablespoons olive oil
1 bream weighing about 1.35 kg (3 lb), cleaned
1 quantity chermoula (see page 42)
1 carrot, cut into matchsticks
2 sticks celery, cut into matchsticks
peel of ½ preserved lemon (see page 10), cut into
   strips
fresh parsley, to garnish

Preheat the oven to 250C (475F/Gas 9). Place the tomatoes in an ovenproof dish, cut side up. Sprinkle with sugar, salt and pepper.

Drizzle the tomatoes with the olive oil and roast in the oven for 30-40 minutes until soft and slightly charred. Rub the fish, inside and out, with the chermoula. Place in a dish and leave in a cool place for 30 minutes. Arrange the carrot and celery in the bottom of a tagine or ovenproof dish. Place the fish on top of the carrot and celery. Add any remaining chermoula and arrange the tomatoes and lemon peel round the sides.

Reduce the oven temperature to 200C (400F/Gas 6). Cover the dish with a lid or foil and bake in the oven for 30 minutes. Remove the foil and spoon any juices over the fish. Return to the oven, uncovered, and cook for a further 10 minutes, or until the fish flakes easily when tested with a knife, and most of the liquid has evaporated. Serve, garnished with parsley.

Serves 4.

— SALMON & COUSCOUS CAKES —

115 g (4 oz/⅔ cup) couscous
225 g (8 oz) salmon fillet, skinned and boned
½ bunch spring onions (scallions), chopped
1½ teaspoons cumin seeds, toasted and ground
2 teaspoons lemon juice
2 tablespoons chopped fresh coriander
1 egg, beaten
3 tablespoons Greek yogurt
2 tablespoons vegetable oil
YELLOW TOMATO & PEPPER SALSA
1 orange pepper (capsicum), seeded and quartered
4 yellow tomatoes, cut in quarters and seeded
½ bunch spring onions (scallions), chopped
juice of ½ lemon
4 tablespoons chopped fresh coriander
salt and freshly ground black pepper

To make the salsa, grill the pepper (capsicum) quarters, skin side up, for 5 minutes until skin blisters and chars. Place in a plastic bag until cool enough to handle, then remove skin. Cut the tomatoes and pepper (capsicum) into fine dice and place in a bowl with the spring onions (scallions), lemon juice, coriander, salt and pepper. Stir salsa and chill until ready to serve. Place couscous in a bowl, add 175 ml (6 fl oz/¾ cup) hot water and leave for 10-15 minutes until water is absorbed.

Put 3 cm (1½ in) water in a frying pan; season with salt and bring to a simmer. Add salmon and poach gently for 5 minutes until fish flakes easily when tested with a knife. Drain and cool, then flake into the couscous. Stir in spring onions (scallions), cumin, lemon juice, coriander, egg, yogurt, salt and pepper. Form into 8 cakes and chill for 30 minutes. In a frying pan, heat the oil and fry the cakes for 5 minutes on each side or until brown. Serve with the salsa and with salad leaves.

Serves 4.

SWORDFISH KEBABS

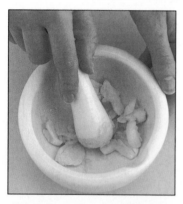

700g (1½lbs) skinless boneless swordfish steaks
CHERMOULA
4 cloves garlic
1 teaspoon salt
juice 2 lemons
1 tablespoon ground cumin
2 teaspoons paprika
1 fresh red chilli, cored, seeded and roughly chopped
15g (½oz) fresh coriander
15g (½oz) fresh parsley
55ml (2floz/¼ cup) olive oil

To make the chermoula, in a mortar and pestle, crush the garlic with the salt. Place in a
blender or food processor.

Add the lemon juice to the food processor
with the cumin, paprika, red chilli, coriander
and parsley. Process briefly then gradually
add the olive oil and reduce to a coarse
purée. Transfer to a bowl. Cut the swordfish
into 2.5cm (1in) cubes and add to the chermoula mixture. Mix well to coat, cover and
leave in a cool place for 1 hour.

Thread the fish onto skewers and place on a
rack over a grill pan. Spoon the marinade
over the fish. Grill under a preheated grill,
close to the heat, for 3-4 minutes on each
side, until the fish is lightly browned and
flakes easily when tested with a knife. Serve
with Tomato, Olive & Caper Salad (see
page 83) and warm pitta bread.

Serves 4.

Variation: Fish such as monkfish, or raw
tiger prawns may be used for this recipe.

—MOROCCAN SEAFOOD PILAFF—

700g (1½lb) mixed fresh shellfish e.g. squid, prawns
  and scallops, cleaned
225g (8oz) skinless cod fillet, cut into bite sized
  pieces
1 quantity chermoula (see page 42)
700g (1½lb) mussels in their shells
2 tablespoons vegetable oil
2 sticks celery, sliced
2 red peppers (capsicums), seeded and chopped
1 onion, chopped
300g (10oz) long grain rice
550ml (20floz/2½ cups) fish stock
400g can chopped tomatoes
salt and freshly ground black pepper
coriander sprigs and lemon slices, to garnish

Cut the squid into 5mm (¼in) rings, shell
the prawns and halve the scallops. Place the
shellfish in a bowl with the cod, add the
chermoula and mix well. Cover and refrigerate for 1 hour. Scrub the mussels, discarding
any open ones; cover and refrigerate. Heat
the oil in a large sauté pan. Add the celery
and peppers (capsicums) and fry for 3 minutes, then remove and set aside. Add the
onion and cook for 10 minutes until soft.
Stir in the rice then add the stock. Drain the
fish and add the marinade to the pan with
the tomatoes, salt and pepper.

Bring to the boil, cover and simmer gently
for 30 minutes, stirring occasionally, until
the rice is cooked and the liquid is almost
absorbed. Add more stock, if necessary.
Return the celery and peppers (capsicums)
to the pan. Place the fish and the mussels on
top. Cover and simmer for 10 minutes, or
until the fish is cooked and the mussels have
opened. Discard any unopened mussels.
Leave to stand, covered, for 10 minutes.
Serve, garnished with coriander and lemon.

Serves 6-8.

MOROCCAN PRAWNS

450 g (1lb) raw peeled tiger prawns
2 cloves garlic, crushed
1 teaspoon paprika
1 teaspoon ground cumin
½ teaspoon ground coriander
¼ teaspoon cayenne pepper
2 tablespoons olive oil
½ bunch spring onions (scallions), finely sliced
2 tablespoons chopped fresh coriander
AVOCADO & MELON SALSA
1 ripe avocado
juice 1 lime
225 g (8 oz) melon, seeded and cut into small dice
½ bunch spring onions (scallions), finely chopped
1 fresh red chilli, cored, seeded and finely chopped
salt

To make the salsa, cut the avocado in half, remove the stone and peel off the skin. Dice the flesh finely and place in a bowl. Add the lime juice and mix well. Add the diced melon, spring onions (scallions), chilli and salt to taste. Cover and leave to stand for 30 minutes.

If necessary, remove the heads and tails from the prawns and de-vein. Rinse and pat dry with kitchen paper. In a bowl, mix together the garlic, salt, paprika, cumin, ground coriander and cayenne. Add the prawns and mix well. In a large frying pan, heat the oil. Add the prawns and spring onions (scallions) and stir fry for 5 minutes or until the prawns are pink and cooked through. Stir in the chopped coriander. Serve with the salsa and with rice.

Serves 4.

—SQUID WITH SAFFRON SAUCE—

450g (1 lb) small squid
1 tablespoon vegetable oil
1 fennel bulb, very thinly sliced
2 tablespoons chopped fresh parsley
2 tablespoons chopped sun-dried tomatoes
juice of ½ lemon
SAFFRON SAUCE
150 ml (5 fl oz/⅔ cup) fish stock
4 saffron threads
150 ml (5 fl oz/⅔ cup) mayonnaise
salt and freshly ground black pepper

To make the saffron sauce, boil the fish stock until reduced to 1 tablespoon. Add the saffron threads. Leave to cool.

Strain stock into a bowl and stir in mayonnaise. Season with salt, pepper and lemon juice. Clean the squid. Pull on tentacles; cut off just above the head, discarding head and innards. Slip quill like transparent bone out of body. Rinse body inside and out, pulling away pink outer membrane. Dry on kitchen paper. Cut body into 0.5 cm (¼in) rings and cut the tentacles into small pieces.

In a frying pan, heat the oil. Add the squid and sauté for a minute or until it becomes opaque. Season with salt and pepper. Drain and set aside to cool. In a serving bowl, arrange the fennel, parsley and sun-dried tomatoes. Add the squid and pour the lemon juice over. Serve with the saffron sauce.

Serves 4.

—PRAWN & COUSCOUS SALAD—

5 tablespoons olive oil
2 shallots, finely chopped
350 ml (12 fl oz/1½ cups) chicken stock
115 g (4 oz) shelled fresh peas
225 g (8 oz/1¼ cups) couscous
2 teaspoons lemon juice
salt and freshly ground black pepper
320 g (11 oz) cooked prawns
fresh mint, to garnish
HARISSA
12 dried red chillies
1 tablespoon coriander seeds
2 teaspoons cumin seeds
2 cloves garlic
½ teaspoon salt
4-6 tablespoons olive oil

To make the harissa, discard the stems and seeds from the chillies, then place in a bowl and cover with boiling water. Leave to soak for 30 minutes until softened. In a heavy based frying pan, heat the coriander and cumin seeds until they smell aromatic. Grind to a powder in a grinder. Drain the chillies and place in a blender with the garlic, coriander mixture and salt. Blend together, trickling in the olive oil until the sauce has a mayonnaise-like consistency. In a pan, heat 2 tablespoons of the oil. Fry the shallots for 10 minutes until soft.

Add 1-2 teaspoons of harissa, the stock and peas. Bring to the boil. Remove from the heat and stir in the couscous. Leave for 10 minutes, until the stock is absorbed. Transfer to a shallow dish and leave to cool. In a bowl, whisk the lemon juice, remaining oil, salt and pepper; stir into couscous with the prawns. Serve warm, garnished with mint.

Serves 4.

Note: To store the harissa, transfer to a screw-top jar and pour olive oil over the top.

CHICKEN TAGINE

2 lemons
2 tablespoons vegetable oil, plus oil for frying
1 onion, chopped
1.5 kg (3¼-3½lb) chicken, cut into pieces
1 teaspoon ground cumin
1 teaspoon ground paprika
1 teaspoon ground ginger
large pinch saffron threads, crushed
1 cinnamon stick
salt and freshly ground black pepper
55 g (2 oz/⅓ cup) pitted green olives
peel from 1 preserved lemon (see page 10), cut into
    strips
2 tablespoons chopped fresh coriander
1 tablespoon chopped fresh parsley
harissa (see page 46), to serve

With a zester, remove rind from the lemons and place in a bowl. Squeeze the juice over and set aside. In a heavy based casserole, heat the oil. Add the onion and cook for 10 minutes until soft. Remove the onion and add the chicken. Cook until browned all over. Stir in the cumin, paprika, ginger, saffron and cinnamon stick. Cook for 1 minute then return the onions to the casserole. Pour in 250 ml (9 fl oz/1 cup) water. Season with salt and pepper and bring to the boil. Cover and simmer gently for 45 minutes.

Stir in the olives, preserved lemon, coriander and parsley and cook for a further 10-15 minutes until the chicken is cooked. Meanwhile, drain the lemon rind and pat dry with kitchen paper. In a small saucepan, heat 1 cm (½in) oil. Add the rind, which will crisp almost immediately. Quickly drain off the oil through a sieve. Serve the chicken and sauce with the fried lemon rind scattered over. Serve with bread, and with the harissa handed separately.

Serves 6.

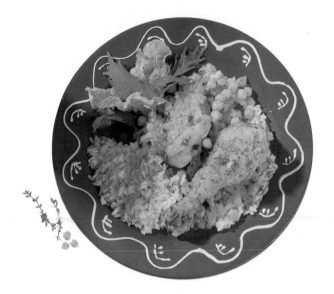

– SAFFRON CHICKEN CASSEROLE –

115 g (4 oz/¾ cup) chick-peas
½ teaspoon paprika
½ teaspoon each ground cumin and ground coriander
salt and freshly ground black pepper
2 kg (4½lb) chicken, cut into serving pieces
55 g (2 oz) butter
1 tablespoon vegetable oil
2 large mild onions, thinly sliced
½ teaspoon saffron threads
about 1 litre (35 fl oz/4½ cups) chicken stock
1 sprig thyme
4 tablespoons chopped fresh parsley
225 g (8 oz/1½ cups) rice, to serve

Place chick-peas in a bowl. Cover with cold water and leave overnight to soak.

Drain the chick-peas and place in a saucepan, cover with water and bring to the boil. Boil for 1 hour. In a bowl, mix together the paprika, cumin, coriander, salt and pepper. Toss the chicken pieces in the mixture. Heat the butter and oil in a large flameproof casserole. Add the chicken pieces and sauté until browned. Transfer to a plate. Add the onions to the casserole and cook for 10 minutes until soft. Return the chicken pieces to the casserole and add the chick-peas. Add the saffron threads to the stock.

Pour over enough stock to cover the chicken and bring to the boil. Add the thyme. Cover and simmer gently for about 1 hour or until the chicken is tender. Stir in the chopped parsley and check the seasoning. Meanwhile, cook the rice in boiling salted water. To serve, drain the rice and arrange half of it a heated serving dish. Place the chicken and onions on top and pour over as much saffron sauce as desired. Add the remaining rice and serve with salad.

Serves 6.

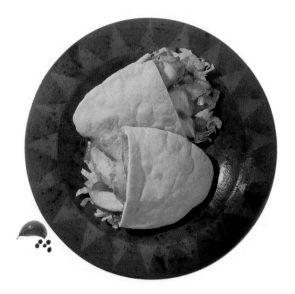

– MOROCCAN CHICKEN IN PITTA –

100 ml (3½fl oz) Greek yogurt
2 teaspoons harissa (see page 46)
2 teaspoons each ground cumin and ground coriander
2 cloves garlic, crushed
1 tablespoon olive oil
salt and freshly ground black pepper
4 boneless skinless chicken breasts
pitta bread, shredded lettuce and chopped tomatoes,
    to serve

In a bowl, mix together the yogurt, harissa, cumin, coriander, garlic, olive oil, salt and pepper. Spread over the chicken breasts and place in a dish. Cover the dish and place in the refrigerator for 2 hours.

Preheat the oven to 200C (400F/Gas 6). Place the chicken breasts on a grid in a roasting tin and cook in the oven for 25 minutes until browned and the juices run clear when pierced with a knife. Place the pitta bread in the oven for the last 5 minutes of cooking, to warm through.

To serve, cut the chicken into thin slices. Cut the pitta bread in half and open to form pockets; fill the pockets with the sliced chicken, shredded lettuce and chopped tomatoes.

Serves 4-6.

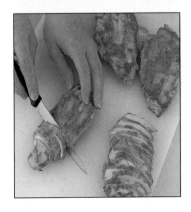

— TUNISIAN SPICED POUSSIN —

2 poussins
25 g (1 oz/2 tablespoons) butter
2 teaspoons paprika
2 teaspoons each clear honey and tomato purée (paste)
4 tablespoons lemon juice
150 ml (5 fl oz/⅔ cup) chicken stock
1 teaspoon harissa (see page 46)
STUFFING
25 g (1 oz/2 tablespoons) butter
1 onion, chopped
2 cloves garlic, crushed
1 teaspoon each ground cinnamon and ground cumin
25 g (1 oz) blanched almonds, finely chopped
175 g (6 oz) mixed ready-to-eat dried fruit, chopped
salt and freshly ground black pepper

To make the stuffing, melt the butter in a saucepan. Add the onion and garlic and cook gently for 10 minutes until soft. Add the cinnamon and cumin and cook, stirring, for 2 minutes. Add the almonds and fruit, season with salt and pepper and cook for 2 minutes. Leave to cool. Preheat the oven to 200C (400F/Gas 6). Stuff the neck end of the poussins with the stuffing. Set aside any excess. In a small saucepan, melt the butter with the paprika; brush over the poussins. Place in a roasting tin and roast for 45-60 minutes, basting occasionally, until cooked.

Transfer the poussins to a carving board. Pour any excess fat from the roasting tin. Stir the honey, tomato purée (paste), lemon juice, stock and harissa into the juices in the tin. Add salt to taste. Bring to the boil and simmer for 2 minutes. Reheat any excess stuffing. Serve the poussins with the stuffing and sauce, and with parsley rice.

Serves 4.

——DUCK TAGINE WITH PEARS——

1 tablespoon olive oil
3 duck breasts, about 1 kg (2¼lb) total weight
4 onions, thinly sliced
3 cloves garlic, crushed
1 teaspoon sugar
2 teaspoons ground cinnamon
½ teaspoon saffron threads
400 ml (14 fl oz/1¾ cups) chicken stock
salt and freshly ground black pepper
115 g (4 oz/¾ cup) ready-to-eat dried pears
3 tablespoons chopped fresh coriander

Heat the oil in a large non-stick frying pan (skillet). Add the duck, skin side up, and cook for 1-2 minutes until lightly browned.

Turn the duck breasts and cook, as gently as possible, until the skin is brown and crisp. Remove and drain on kitchen paper. Pour off all but 3 tablespoons of fat. Add the onions and cook for 15 minutes until completely soft. Slice the duck breasts across into 1 cm (½in) slices. Place the onion and duck in a heavy flameproof casserole.

Stir in the garlic, sugar, cinnamon, saffron and stock. Season with salt and pepper. Cover and simmer gently for 30 minutes. Cut the pears into pieces, add to the casserole, cover and cook gently for a further 30 minutes. Stir in the coriander and serve with couscous.

Serves 6.

─────── BISTILLA ───────

1 carrot, coarsely chopped
2 onions, 1 coarsely chopped, 1 finely chopped
2 pigeons
1 bay leaf
6 peppercorns
100 g (3½oz) butter
55 g (2 oz/⅓ cup) blanched almonds, finely chopped
2 teaspoons caster sugar
½ teaspoon ground cinnamon
3 tablespoons chopped fresh parsley
4 eggs, lightly beaten
salt and freshly ground black pepper
12 sheets filo pastry, 40x30cm (16x12 in)
icing sugar and ground cinnamon, to decorate

Place the carrot and coarsely chopped onion in a flameproof casserole with the pigeons, bay leaf and peppercorns. Add enough water to cover. Bring to the boil, cover and simmer gently for 45-60 minutes until the pigeons are very tender. Remove from the casserole and set aside to cool. Strain the stock and reserve, discarding the vegetables. When the pigeons are cool enough to handle, cut the breasts away from the carcass. Remove the skin and cut the meat into small pieces. Set the pigeon meat aside.

Heat 15 g (½oz) butter in a small frying pan. Add the almonds and cook, stirring, for a minute, or until light golden. Transfer to a bowl. When cool, stir in the caster sugar and ground cinnamon. Place the finely chopped onion in a saucepan with the parsley and 150 ml (5 fl oz/⅔ cup) of the reserved stock. Bring to the boil, cover and simmer for 15 minutes or until the onion is soft. Remove the lid and cook briskly until the liquid has evaporated. Set aside to cool.

Whisk 2 tablespoons of the reserved stock into the lightly beaten eggs. Season with salt and pepper. Heat 25g (1oz) of the butter in a saucepan. Add the egg mixture and stir over a gentle heat until just set but still creamy. Preheat the oven to 180C (350F/ Gas 4).

In a small saucepan, melt the remaining butter. Unwrap the filo sheets and keep loosely covered with cling film until required. Cut 2 sheets of filo widthways in half. Brush one half-sheet with melted butter. Place a second half-sheet on top and brush with butter. Repeat with the remaining two half-sheets. Press the buttered filo sheets into a 10cm (4in) loose bottomed flan tin allowing the excess to overhang the edge. Repeat with 5 more flan tins. Divide the egg mixture between the 6 flan tins. Cover with a layer of onion mixture, then almond mixture.

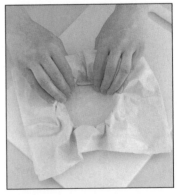

Arrange the pigeon meat on top and sprinkle 1 teaspoon of reserved stock over each pie. Trim the corners of the overhanging pastry then fold the pastry over the top of the pies, pressing down firmly. Brush each pie with melted butter. Bake in the oven for 30 minutes until golden and crisp. Serve, sprinkled with icing sugar and ground cinnamon, with a mixed salad.

Serves 6.

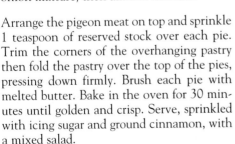

QUAIL WITH GRAPES

5 cm (2 in) fresh root ginger, peeled and finely
  chopped
8 quail
55 g (2 oz) butter
salt and freshly ground black pepper
175 g (6 oz) seedless white grapes, halved
250 ml (9 fl oz/1 cup) unsweetened white grape juice
1 teaspoon cornflour (cornstarch)
fresh flat leaf parsley, to garnish

Preheat the oven to 220C (425F/Gas 7).
Place some chopped ginger inside each quail.
In a roasting dish, heat the butter. Add the
quail and turn in the butter until browned all
over. Season with salt and pepper.

Roast in the oven for 20 minutes, basting
occasionally, until the quail are browned and
cooked through. Tilt the birds to let the pan
juices run back into the pan. Transfer to a
heated serving dish and keep warm.

Pour any fat from the roasting dish. Add the
grapes and grape juice and place over the
heat. Simmer for a few minutes, scraping up
the sediment, until the grapes are warm. In a
bowl, blend the cornflour (cornstarch) with
a little cold water and stir into the sauce.
Simmer until thickened. Season with salt
and pepper. Arrange the grapes round the
quail and pour the sauce round. Serve with
bulgar wheat or rice, garnished with flat leaf
parsley.

Serves 4.

–GRILLED QUAIL & ARAB SALAD–

8 quail
70 ml (2½fl oz/⅓ cup) olive oil
juice of 2 lemons
4 cloves garlic, crushed
salt and freshly ground black pepper
2 tablespoons chopped fresh parsley
ARAB SALAD
1 teaspoon harissa (see page 46)
5 tablespoons olive oil
2 tablespoons lemon juice
225 g (8 oz) cherry tomatoes, halved
1 small or ½ large cucumber, cut into cubes
1 bunch spring onions (scallions), chopped
1 bunch watercress, washed and dried

With a pair of kitchen scissors, cut the quail down the backbone, turn them over and press down on the breastbone to flatten them out. Pat dry with kitchen paper. Pass two skewers through each quail. Place them in a glass dish. In a bowl, mix together the olive oil, lemon juice, garlic, salt and pepper and parsley. Pour over the quail. Cover and marinate in the refrigerator for 4-6 hours.

To make the salad, in a bowl, mix together the harissa, olive oil, lemon juice, salt and pepper. Add the tomatoes, cucumber, spring onions (scallions), and watercress. Mix lightly. Remove the quail from the marinade and place on the grill rack. Grill under a pre-heated grill for 10-15 minutes, turning during cooking and brushing with the marinade. Serve with the salad.

Serves 4.

—GUINEA FOWL IN BEETROOT—

450g (1 lb) uncooked beetroot (beets)
1 onion, chopped
400 ml (14 fl oz/1¾ cups) chicken stock
45 g (1½oz) butter
1 teaspoon ground cumin
½ teaspoon each ground allspice and ground cinnamon
1 guinea fowl, quartered
salt and freshly ground black pepper
1 teaspoon cornflour (cornstarch)
4 tablespoons natural yogurt
chopped fresh mint, to garnish

Place the beetroot (beets) in a pan of boiling water. Cover and simmer for 30-60 minutes until tender. Drain.

Preheat the oven to 170C (325F/Gas 3). As soon as the beetroot (beets) are cool enough to handle, remove the skin. Cut the beetroot (beets) into chunks and place in a blender or food processor with the onion and chicken stock. Blend until completely smooth. In a flameproof casserole, melt the butter. Add the cumin, allspice and cinnamon and cook for 1 minute. Add the guinea fowl portions and cook until lightly browned.

Stir in the beetroot (beet) purée and season with salt and pepper. Heat to simmering point then cover and cook in the oven for 1 hour or until the guinea fowl is very tender. Place the guinea fowl on a heated serving plate. Blend the cornflour (cornstarch) with a little cold water and pour into the sauce. Bring to the boil and simmer for a minute until slightly thickened. Pour the sauce over the guinea fowl; drizzle the yogurt over and scatter with chopped mint. Serve with rice.

Serves 4.

–MEATBALLS IN TOMATO SAUCE–

450g (1 lb) lean minced beef
1 medium onion, grated
1 clove garlic, crushed
2 tablespoons fresh breadcrumbs
1 tablespoon chopped fresh parsley
1 tablespoon chopped fresh mint
½ teaspoon each ground cinnamon and ground coriander
salt and freshly ground black pepper
flour for dusting
2 tablespoons vegetable oil
TOMATO SAUCE
1 tablespoon olive oil
1 onion, finely chopped
1 clove garlic, crushed
400g (14oz) can chopped tomatoes
1 teaspoon sugar

To make the sauce, heat the olive oil in a saucepan. Add the onion and garlic and cook for 10 minutes until soft. Add the tomatoes, sugar, salt and pepper. Simmer for 5 minutes. In a blender or food processor, process the sauce until fairly smooth. Return to the saucepan and set aside.

In a large bowl, mix together the beef, onion, garlic, breadcrumbs, parsley, mint, cinnamon, coriander, salt and pepper. On a floured board, roll the mixture into small balls. In a frying pan (skillet), heat the vegetable oil and fry the meatballs until browned all over and firm. Add to the tomato sauce and simmer for 20 minutes until tender. Serve with rice garnished with mint.

Serves 4.

—— MOROCCAN BROCHETTES ——

1 onion, roughly chopped
2 cloves garlic, roughly chopped
1 fresh red chilli, seeded and cut into strips
700g (1½lb) minced beef
4 tablespoons chopped fresh parsley
½ teaspoon dried oregano
1 teaspoon each paprika and ground cumin
1 teaspoon salt
½ teaspoon freshly ground black pepper
yogurt and chopped spring onions (scallions), to serve

Place the onion, garlic and chilli in a food processor and process briefly. Add the minced beef, parsley, oregano, paprika, cumin, salt and pepper and blend to a paste.

Transfer the mixture to a bowl, cover and leave to stand for 30 minutes. With damp hands, take an egg-sized piece of the mixture and press it into a long sausage shape on a skewer. (Skewers made from rosemary twigs may be used to add extra fragrance.)

Grill the brochettes under the grill or on a barbecue, turning frequently, for 6-7 minutes, until well browned on the outside but still moist inside. To serve, spoon yogurt over the brochettes and sprinkle with chopped spring onions (scallions). Serve with salad and pitta bread.

Serves 6.

— BEEF TAGINE WITH PRUNES —

225 (8oz/1¼ cups) pitted prunes
1 teaspoon ground ginger
1 tablespoon ground coriander
pinch saffron threads
salt and freshly ground black pepper
3 tablespoons olive oil
1.25 kg (2¾lb) stewing beef, cubed
2 onions, sliced
2 cloves garlic, crushed
chicken stock or water
1 cinnamon stick
1 tablespoon clear honey
1 teaspoon harissa (see page 46)
1 tablespoon sesame seeds
3 tablespoons chopped fresh parsley
1 teaspoon orange flower water, to serve

Place the prunes in a bowl and cover with boiling water. Leave to soak for 2 hours. In a large bowl, mix together the ginger, coriander, saffron, salt, pepper and 2 tablespoons of the oil. Add the beef and mix well, rubbing the spices into the meat with your fingers. Transfer to a tagine or casserole. In a large frying pan (skillet), heat the remaining oil. Add the onions and garlic and cook for 10 minutes until soft. Add to the spiced beef, then pour in enough stock or water to barely cover the meat. Add the cinnamon stick.

Cover the tagine and simmer gently for 2 hours until the beef is tender. Check from time to time and add more liquid, if necessary. Drain the prunes and add to the casserole; simmer for 20 minutes longer. Stir in the honey and harissa and cook for a further 15 minutes. Dry fry the sesame seeds in a frying pan (skillet) until lightly browned. To serve, stir in the parsley, sprinkle with orange flower water and scatter the sesame seeds on top. Serve with couscous.

Serves 6.

-LAMB BURGERS & MINT RELISH-

450g (1lb) lean minced lamb
1 small onion, finely chopped
1 clove garlic, crushed
1 teaspoon each ground cumin and ground coriander
1 teaspoon harissa (see page 46)
1 tablespoon chopped fresh parsley
olive oil for brushing
pitta bread and salad, to serve
MINT RELISH
45g (1½oz) fresh mint
15g (½oz) fresh coriander
1 clove garlic, crushed
2 tablespoons lime juice
salt and freshly ground black pepper
1 teaspoon sugar
2 tablespoons olive oil

To make the mint relish, reserve 4 sprigs of mint for garnish. Place the mint, coriander, garlic, lime juice, salt, pepper, sugar and half the olive oil in a blender or food processor and process for 1 minute; scrape down the sides of the bowl and process again to a paste. Transfer to a bowl and pour the remaining oil on top to prevent the paste from discolouring.

Mix together the lamb, onion, garlic, cumin, coriander, harissa, parsley and salt until well combined. Shape into four burgers. Heat a ridged grill pan. Brush the burgers with olive oil and cook for 3 minutes on each side for medium rare or 5 minutes for well done. (For beef, cook to well done.) To serve, split the pitta breads, place some salad on the bottom and then the burgers. Put a spoonful of the mint relish on each burger and garnish with the reserved mint leaves.

Serves 4.

—LAMB KEBABS WITH SALSA—

2 cloves garlic, crushed
4 tablespoons lemon juice
2 tablespoons olive oil
1 dried red chilli, crushed
1 teaspoon ground cumin
1 teaspoon ground coriander
575 g (1¼lb) lean lamb, cut into 4 cm (1½in) cubes
salt and freshly ground black pepper
8 bay leaves
peel of ½ preserved lemon (see page 10), cut up
TOMATO & OLIVE SALSA
175 g (6oz/1¼ cups) mixed pitted olives, chopped
1 small red onion, finely chopped
4 plum tomatoes, peeled and chopped
1 fresh red chilli, cored, seeded and finely chopped
2 tablespoons olive oil

Mix the garlic, lemon juice, olive oil, chilli, cumin and coriander in a large shallow dish. Add the lamb cubes, with pepper to taste. Mix well. Cover and leave to marinate in the refrigerator for 2 hours. To make the salsa, put the olives, onion, tomatoes, chilli, olive oil, salt and pepper in a bowl. Mix well, cover and set aside.

Remove the lamb from the marinade and divide among 4 skewers, adding the bay leaves and lemon peel at intervals. Grill over a barbecue, on a ridged iron grill pan or under a hot grill, turning occasionally, for 10 minutes until the lamb is browned and crisp outside and pink and juicy inside. Serve with the salsa, and with savoury rice.

Serves 4.

Variation: Lean beef may be used instead of lamb but should be cooked to well done.

——— MOROCCAN COUSCOUS ———

1 kg (2¼lb) trimmed lamb shoulder, cut into pieces
2 onions, chopped
55 g (2 oz/⅓ cup) chick-peas, soaked overnight
1 teaspoon ground ginger
salt and freshly ground black pepper
pinch saffron threads
4 each small turnips and carrots, in large pieces
450 g (1 lb/2½ cups) regular couscous (not instant)
25 g (1 oz) smen or butter, melted
a little rosewater
55 g (2 oz/⅓ cup) raisins
4 medium courgettes (zucchini), halved lengthways
1 butternut squash, peeled and cubed
2 tomatoes, quartered
2 tablespoons each chopped fresh coriander and parsley

Place the lamb, with the onions and chick-peas in the bottom of a couscoussière or large stockpot. Stir in the ginger, saffron and 1 teaspoon pepper. Cover with water, bring to the boil and simmer, covered, for 45 minutes. Add the turnips and carrots.

Place the couscous grains in a large bowl. Dissolve 1 teaspoon salt in 150ml (5 fl oz/ ⅔ cup) water and sprinkle over the couscous. Stir with your fingers, rubbing to separate the grains and break up any lumps. When the couscous has soaked up all the water, place in the top of a couscoussière, or in a colander lined with muslin. Set the couscoussière or colander on top of the simmering stew.

If any steam escapes, wrap a strip of cloth around the top of the pan before placing the couscous on top. Steam, covered, for 20 minutes, occasionally drawing a fork through the couscous grains to separate them. Turn the couscous out onto a large wooden or earthenware dish. Sprinkle with a little salted water, as before, and separate the grains with your fingers.

Lightly rub in the melted smen or butter and the rosewater and put the couscous back in the top part of the couscoussière or colander. Add the raisins, courgettes (zucchini), squash, tomatoes, salt, coriander and parsley to the simmering stew then replace the couscous over the pan. Steam for a further 30 minutes, occasionally fluffing the couscous grains with a fork.

To serve, pile the couscous onto a large wooden or earthenware serving dish. With a slotted spoon, transfer the lamb and vegetables to to the centre of the dish. Pour over some of the broth. Stir some harissa (see page 46) into the remaining broth and serve it separately.

Serves 6.

Variation: The selection of vegetables can include beans, peas, aubergine (eggplant), but traditionally seven vegetables are used.

POMEGRANATE LAMB

3 tablespoons vegetable oil
1 large onion, sliced
2 cloves garlic, finely chopped
2.5 cm (1 in) piece fresh root ginger, peeled and
    finely chopped
1 kg (2¼lb) lean lamb such as shoulder or leg, cubed
salt and freshly ground black pepper
juice of 2 pomegranates, about 300 ml (10 fl oz/
    1¼ cups)
1 teaspoon ground cumin
½ teaspoon ground cinnamon
¼ teaspoon ground nutmeg
3 cardamom pods, lightly crushed
85 ml (3 fl oz) Greek yogurt
pomegranate seeds and chopped fresh mint, to garnish

Heat the oil in a large flameproof casserole. Add the onion, garlic and ginger and cook for 10 minutes until soft. Remove from the pan and set aside. In the same pan, brown the lamb, in batches, and set aside. Return the onion, garlic, ginger and lamb to the pan. Season with salt and pepper. Gradually stir in the pomegranate juice, allowing each addition to be absorbed before adding more. There should be very little liquid left.

Add the cumin, cinnamon, nutmeg and cardamom to the pan and stir for 1 minute. Stir in the yogurt. Cover the pan tightly and cook very gently, preferably on a heat diffuser, for 30-40 minutes until the lamb is tender. Check from time to time that the meat is not sticking and drying out too much. Add a little water, if necessary. Garnish with pomegranate seeds and chopped mint, and serve with rice.

Serves 4-6.

—ROAST STUFFED LEG OF LAMB—

1.8 kg (4 lb) boned leg of lamb, plus the bones
salt and freshly ground black pepper
1 onion, quartered
7 tablespoons olive oil
3 rosemary sprigs
150 ml (5 fl oz/⅔ cup) dry white wine
juice of 2 lemons
STUFFING
55 g (2 oz/¼ cup) couscous
2 tablespoons olive oil
1 small onion, finely chopped
1 clove garlic, crushed
1 teaspoon ground cinnamon
1 teaspoon ground cumin
115 g (4 oz/1 cup) ready-to-eat dried apricots, chopped
55 g (2 oz/⅔ cup) pine nuts

To make the stuffing, place the couscous in a bowl and cover with boiling water; leave to stand until absorbed and fluff up with a fork. Heat the oil, add the onion and garlic and cook for 10 minutes. Leave to cool. Stir into the couscous with the cinnamon, cumin, apricots, pine nuts, salt and pepper. Place 5 pieces of string in parallel lines on the work surface. Place the lamb, skin side down, across them and season with salt and pepper. Spoon the stuffing onto the meat. Roll up firmly and tie to make a neat shape. Preheat the oven to 240C (475F/Gas 9).

Roast the lamb bones and onion in a tin with 3 tablespoons of the oil for 15 minutes. Add the rosemary and lamb. Pour in the wine and lemon juice, spoon over remaining olive oil and season. Roast for 15 minutes, then reduce heat to 220C (400F/Gas 6) and cook for 1 hour, basting occasionally. Remove the lamb and leave to stand for 15 minutes. Add 550 ml (20 fl oz/2½ cups) water to the tin, and boil until reduced. Serve with the lamb. Serve with a mixed salad.

Serves 6-8.

—LAMB & MASHED CHICK-PEAS—

1 clove garlic, crushed
1 teaspoon ground cumin
1 teaspoon ground coriander
1 teaspoon paprika
1 teaspoon dried thyme
2 tablespoons olive oil
Grated rind and juice of 1 lemon
2 racks of lamb, trimmed
MASHED CHICK-PEAS
2 (15-oz.) cans chick-peas, drained
2 cloves garlic, crushed
Juice of ½ lemon
Salt and freshly ground black pepper

In a small bowl, mix together the garlic, cumin, coriander, paprika, thyme, olive oil, lemon rind and juice. Place the lamb in a roasting pan. Spread the spice paste over the lamb and refrigerate 1 hour. Preheat the oven to 425F (220C). Roast the lamb in the oven 25 to 30 minutes for medium rare. Allow an extra 10 minutes for medium and a further 15-20 minutes for well done. Remove the lamb from the oven, cover with foil and allow to stand 5 to 10 minutes.

Meanwhile, make the mashed chick-peas. Place the chick-peas, garlic, lemon juice, salt and pepper in a blender or food processor. Process until smooth, adding a little boiling water to make the desired consistency. Transfer to a saucepan and heat gently. To serve, carve the lamb into individual chops. Place a mound of chick-peas on each of 4 heated plates and arrange the chops on top. Serve with roasted vegetables.

Makes 4 servings.

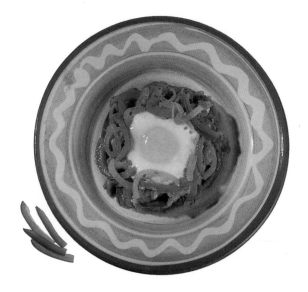

CHAKCHOUKA

2 tablespoons olive oil
1 onion, thinly sliced
1 clove garlic, crushed
1 red pepper (capsicum), seeded and sliced
1 green pepper (capsicum), seeded and sliced
4 merguez sausages, sliced
6 tomatoes, peeled and quartered
salt and freshly ground black pepper
1 teaspoon harissa (see page 46)
2 teaspoons chopped fresh mint
4 eggs

Heat the oil in a large frying pan (skillet). Add the onion, garlic and peppers (capsicum) and cook gently for 10 minutes.

Add the sausages, cook for a few minutes, then stir in the tomatoes. Season with salt, pepper and harissa and cook slowly for 10 more minutes until the vegetables are well blended. Stir in the mint.

Make 4 indentations in the mixture and break an egg into each one. Cover the pan and cook gently for 6-7 minutes until the eggs are set. Divide into 4 and serve straight from the pan.

Serves 4.

Variation: The eggs may be omitted and double the quantity of sausages used instead.

—BULGAR & VERMICELLI PILAFF—

2 tablespoons olive oil
1 onion, thinly sliced
1 green pepper (capsicum), seeded and sliced
25 g (1 oz) cut vermicelli
225 g (8 oz/1¼ cups) bulgar wheat
350 ml (12 fl oz/1½ cups) vegetable stock
2 tomatoes, roughly chopped
salt and freshly ground black pepper
2 tablespoons chopped fresh flat leaved parsley
fried onions, to garnish

Heat the olive oil in a large saucepan. Add the onion and cook for 5 minutes then add the sliced pepper (capsicum) and cook until the onion is soft.

Add the vermicelli and stir to coat with oil. Put the bulgar wheat in a colander and rinse in cold water, then add to the pan. Pour in the vegetable stock and bring to the boil. Cover the pan and simmer for 5 minutes.

Add the tomatoes and simmer for a further 5-10 minutes until the bulgar wheat is tender and the stock is absorbed. Add more stock if necessary. Season with salt and pepper and stir in the parsley. Serve, garnished with fried onions.

Serves 6.

MOROCCAN RICE

350g (12oz/2¼ cups) long grain rice
55g (2oz) butter
pinch of saffron threads
salt and freshly ground black pepper
½ cinnamon stick
45g (1½oz) ready-to-eat dried apricots, chopped
45g (1½oz) raisins
25g (1oz) hazelnuts
25g (1oz) pine nuts

Place the rice in a bowl and cover with plenty of water. Leave to soak for 1 hour. Drain, rinse under cold water and drain again. Spread out on a tray to dry for 30 minutes.

Melt ¾ of the butter in a large heavy saucepan. Stir in the rice and saffron. Pour 850ml (30floz/3¾ cups) water over, add 1 teaspoon salt and the cinnamon stick and bring to the boil. Stir in the apricots and raisins and bring to the boil. Cover the pan then simmer on the lowest heat, without removing the lid, for 15 minutes or until the rice is tender and the liquid is absorbed. Remove from the heat.

Cover the rice with a dry tea towel and leave to stand for 15 minutes. Melt the remaining butter in a small frying pan (skillet) and toss the hazelnuts and pine nuts in it until golden. Season the rice with pepper then stir in the nuts just before serving.

Serves 6.

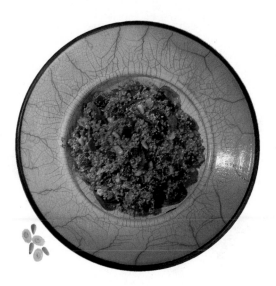

-COUSCOUS & BEETROOT SALAD-

450g (1 lb) couscous
chicken or vegetable stock
juice of 1 lemon
3 tablespoons olive oil, plus extra for drizzling
salt and freshly ground black pepper
300g (10oz) cooked beetroot, cut into 1cm (½in) cubes
4 spring onions (scallions), chopped
70g (2½oz) baby rocket (arugula) leaves
70g (2½oz) toasted pine nuts
1 teaspoon toasted cumin seeds
1 tablespoon chopped fresh mint

Place the couscous in a bowl and pour over enough stock to cover. Set aside for 10 minutes until the liquid is absorbed.

Fluff up the grains of couscous with a fork. Stir in the lemon juice and olive oil and season generously with salt and pepper.

Just before serving, stir the beetroot into the couscous. Add the spring onions (scallions), rocket (arugula) leaves, the pine nuts, cumin seeds and mint. Transfer to a salad bowl and drizzle a little olive oil over.

Serves 6.

RICE & LENTILS

115 g (4 oz/⅔ cup) Puy lentils
115 g (4 oz/¾ cup) long grain rice
25 g (1 oz) butter
1 red onion, finely chopped
1 clove garlic, crushed
1 teaspoon turmeric
2 teaspoons ground coriander
1 teaspoon ground cumin
1 tablespoon tomato purée (paste)
550 ml (20 fl oz/2½ cups) vegetable stock
salt and freshly ground black pepper
1 tablespoon chopped fresh coriander

Place the lentils in a bowl, cover with boiling water and leave for 30 minutes.

Rinse the rice and leave to soak for 30 minutes. Heat the butter in a large saucepan. Add the onion and garlic and cook for 10 minutes until soft. Stir in the turmeric, ground coriander and ground cumin and stir for 1 more minute. Drain the lentils and rice thoroughly. Add to the pan and stir for 1 minute.

Stir the tomato purée (paste) into the stock and pour into the rice mixture; season with plenty of salt and pepper and bring to the boil. Cover and simmer for 20 minutes, or until the lentils are tender and the rice is cooked. All the liquid should have been absorbed. Stir in the fresh coriander and serve immediately.

Serves 4.

OKRA & TOMATOES

450g (1 lb) fresh young okra
55 ml (2 fl oz/¼ cup) olive oil
225g (8 oz) white pearl onions
2 cloves garlic, crushed
1 teaspoon ground coriander
450g (1 lb) tomatoes, peeled and chopped
1 tablespoon lemon juice
salt and freshly ground black pepper
1 teaspoon sugar
chopped fresh parsley, to garnish

Cut the stalks off the okra. Wash the pods, drain and pat dry with kitchen paper. Take care not to pierce the pods.

Heat the oil in a large pan, add the onions and cook, turning frequently, for 10 minutes. Add the garlic and ground coriander and cook for 5 more minutes or until the onions are softened and lightly coloured. Add the okra and turn carefully in the oil. Cook for 5 minutes.

Add the tomatoes, lemon juice, salt, pepper and sugar. Cover the pan and simmer gently for 10 minutes. Remove the lid and cook for a further 10 minutes or until the okra are tender and the sauce is reduced. If the sauce reduces too quickly, add a little water. Garnish with chopped parsley and serve, hot, cold or at room temperature.

Serves 4-6.

—POTATO & CHICK-PEA SALAD—

450g (1lb) small new potatoes
2 tablespoons olive oil
1 onion, sliced
2 cloves garlic, sliced
1 teaspoon cumin seeds
450g (1lb) plum tomatoes, peeled
400g (14oz) can chick-peas, drained
salt and freshly ground black pepper
2 tablespoons roughly chopped fresh mint

Either scrub or peel the potatoes, according to preference. Cut in half unless they are very small. Boil in salted water for 10 minutes or until soft. Drain.

Meanwhile, heat the oil in a large saucepan. Add the onion and cook for 10 minutes until soft and golden brown. Add the garlic and cumin seeds and cook for 3 or 4 minutes. Cut the tomatoes into eighths and add to the pan. Cook for a few minutes until the tomatoes begin to soften.

Add the drained chick-peas and the potatoes. Cook for a few minutes until warmed through. Season with salt and pepper and stir in the mint. Serve hot or cold.

Serves 4-6.

STUFFED VEGETABLES

55 g (2 oz) couscous
6 sun-dried tomatoes in oil, drained and chopped
25 g (1 oz) ready-to-eat dried apricots, chopped
1 tablespoon chopped fresh mint
1 tablespoon pine nuts
4 spring onions (scallions), chopped
½ teaspoon ground ginger
salt and freshly ground pepper
4 baby aubergines (eggplants)
4 courgettes (zucchini)
4 baby red peppers (capsicums)
2 tablespoons olive oil
Greek yogurt, to serve

Place the couscous in a bowl and pour 150 ml (5 fl oz/⅔ cup) boiling water over.

Place the sun-dried tomatoes in a bowl with the apricots, mint, pine nuts, spring onions (scallions), ginger, salt and pepper. Fluff up the couscous with a fork and add to the bowl. Mix together. Bring a saucepan of salted water to the boil. Add the aubergines (eggplants), courgettes (zucchini) and peppers (capsicums) and cook for 3 minutes. Drain. Preheat the oven to 200C (400F/Gas 6). Cut the tops off the aubergines (eggplants) and peppers (capsicums). Cut a strip from one side of each courgette (zucchini).

Hollow out the aubergines (eggplants) and courgettes (zucchini), leaving a shell about 5 mm (¼ in) thick. Roughly chop the flesh and add to the couscous mixture. Core and seed the peppers (capsicums). Stuff the vegetables with the couscous mixture. Place in a baking dish and drizzle with the olive oil. Cover the dish with foil and bake for 15 minutes. Remove the foil and bake for a further 10 minutes or until the vegetables are soft. Serve with yogurt.

Serves 4.

– BLACK-EYED BEANS & SPINACH –

225 g (8 oz/1¼ cups) black-eyed beans, soaked
  overnight
2 bay leaves
3 tablespoons vegetable oil
1 large onion, finely chopped
2 cloves garlic, crushed
1 teaspoon cumin seeds
2 teaspoons ground cumin
1 teaspoon ground coriander
4 plum tomatoes, roughly chopped
salt and freshly ground black pepper
450 g (1 lb) fresh young spinach, washed and dried
4 tablespoons Greek yogurt
2 tablespoons chopped fresh coriander

Drain the black-eyed beans and place in a
saucepan with the bay leaves. Cover with
cold water and bring to the boil. Boil rapidly
for 10 minutes then skim off any scum from
the surface. Cover, and simmer for 30-35
minutes until the beans are tender. Drain,
reserving the cooking liquid. Heat the oil in
a large pan. Add the onion and cook for
10 minutes until soft and lightly coloured.
Add the garlic and cumin seeds and cook
until the seeds begin to pop. Add the
ground cumin and coriander and cook, stirring, for 1 minute.

Add the tomatoes and drained beans and
enough reserved cooking liquid just to
cover. Season generously with salt and pepper and simmer until reduced and the tomatoes are soft. Check the seasoning, adding
more salt, if necessary. Stir in the spinach
and cook until the leaves wilt. Stir in the
yogurt and chopped coriander, bring to the
boil and stir well. Serve immediately.

Serves 6.

Variation: To save time, use canned beans.

FRIED BABY CARROTS

450g (1 lb) baby carrots
3 tablespoons olive oil
1 clove garlic, crushed
1 teaspoon caster sugar
grated rind of 1 lemon
juice of ½ lemon
salt and freshly ground black pepper
2 tablespoons roughly chopped fresh mint
sprigs of mint, to garnish

Scrape the carrots and trim them, leaving some green top. If the carrots are bigger than the width of a finger, halve them lengthways.

Heat the oil in a frying pan (skillet) large enough to take the carrots in a single layer. Add the carrots and cook gently for 15 minutes, shaking frequently. Add the garlic and cook for a further 10 minutes until the carrots are tender and flecked with brown.

Add the sugar and cook for 2 minutes to caramelise slightly. Stir in the lemon rind and juice and season with salt and pepper. Stir in the chopped mint and transfer to a serving dish. Garnish with sprigs of mint.

Serves 4.

——— GRILLED VEGETABLES ———

55 g (2 oz) couscous
1 red pepper (capsicum), seeded and cut into quarters
2 baby courgettes (zucchini), cut in half lengthways
2 baby aubergines (eggplants), cut in half lengthways
1 fennel bulb, cut into quarters
4 patty pan squashes
2 tablespoons olive oil
sprigs of mint and lemon slices, to garnish
MARINADE
150 ml (5 fl oz/⅔ cup) olive oil
1 tablespoon lemon juice
2 cloves garlic, crushed
salt and freshly ground black pepper
1 teaspoon chopped fresh parsley
1 teaspoon chopped fresh mint

Place the couscous in a bowl and cover with boiling water. Leave for 10 minutes to absorb the water then fluff up with a fork and spread out in a dish. Leave for 1 hour to dry. To make the marinade, in a large bowl, mix together the olive oil, lemon juice, garlic, salt, pepper, parsley and mint. Place the red pepper (capsicum) in the bowl with the marinade. Add the courgettes (zucchini), aubergines (eggplants), fennel bulb and squashes. Marinate for 1 hour. Preheat a grill or barbecue.

Grill the vegetables, turning and brushing with the marinade every few minutes, for 10 minutes, or until tender and lightly browned. If using a ridged grill pan, grill them in batches; keep them warm while the remainder are grilling. Heat the olive oil in a frying pan (skillet). Add the couscous and fry, stirring, until golden and crisp. Transfer the vegetables to a heated serving dish and scatter the couscous over. Serve, garnished with mint leaves and lemon slices.

Serves 4.

—SWEET & SOUR COURGETTES—

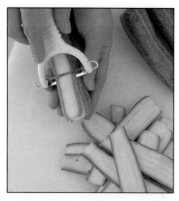

450 g (1 lb) small courgettes (zucchini)
3 tablespoons olive oil
2 cloves garlic, crushed
juice of 1 lemon
2 teaspoons soft brown sugar
3 tablespoons chopped almonds
25 g (1 oz/¼ cup) raisins
salt and freshly ground black pepper
lemon slices, to garnish

Trim the courgettes and cut into long thin slices or ribbons, using a potato peeler.

Heat the oil in a large frying pan (skillet). Add the garlic and cook for 2 minutes. Add the courgettes and stir until coated with oil. Stir in the lemon juice, brown sugar, almonds, raisins, salt and pepper.

Simmer, stirring, for 5-10 minutes, until the courgettes are cooked. If there is too much liquid in the pan, increase the heat for 1-2 minutes to allow it to evaporate. Serve, garnished with lemon slices.

Serves 4.

Variation: Other vegetables such as leeks and baby onions are suitable for cooking in this way.

—MOROCCAN CARROT SALAD—

450 g (1 lb) carrots
2 teaspoons clear honey
3 tablespoons olive oil
juice of ½ lemon
1 tablespoon rosewater
85 g (3 oz/⅓ cup) raisins
½ teaspoon ground cinnamon
salt and freshly ground black pepper
85 g (3 oz/¾ cup) flaked almonds

Peel and trim the carrots and grate coarsely into a bowl.

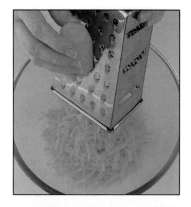

Stir in the honey, olive oil, lemon juice, rosewater, raisins and ground cinnamon. Season with salt and pepper and mix well.

Leave at room temperature for 1 hour for the flavours to blend together. Stir in the flaked almonds and transfer to a serving dish

Serves 4.

—— LENTIL & TOMATO SALAD ——

225 g (8 oz/1¼ cups) green lentils
55 ml (2 fl oz/¼ cup) olive oil
1 onion, finely chopped
2 cloves garlic, crushed
4 plum tomatoes, peeled and chopped
salt and freshly ground black pepper
1 tablespoon chopped fresh parsley
2 tablespoons lemon juice
strips of lemon rind and chopped spring onions
  (scallions), to garnish

Place the lentils in a bowl, cover with cold water and leave to soak for 3-4 hours. Drain well.

Heat half the oil in a large saucepan, add the onion and garlic and cook for 10 minutes or until soft. Add the tomatoes, cook for 1 minute, then add the lentils. Cover with water. Cover the pan and simmer gently for 30 minutes, adding water if necessary, until the lentils are tender and all the water has been absorbed. The lentils should still be holding their shape.

Add salt, pepper, parsley, lemon juice and the remaining oil. Mix carefully, then transfer to a serving dish and leave to cool. Serve, garnished with strips of lemon rind and chopped spring onions (scallions).

Serves 4-6.

-GRILLED AUBERGINES & LABNA-

2 medium aubergines (eggplants), thickly sliced
3 tablespoons olive oil
225 g (8 oz) cherry tomatoes
1 quantity of labna (see page 26)
2 tablespoons toasted pine nuts
sprigs of coriander, to garnish
DRESSING
115 ml (5 fl oz/½ cup) olive oil
juice of 1 lemon
2 tablespoons chopped fresh coriander
salt and freshly ground black pepper

Brush the aubergine slices with olive oil and grill on a pre-heated ridged iron grill pan or under a grill, for 5 minutes or until brown.

Turn, brush with more oil and grill for a few more minutes until tender and browned. Transfer to a serving dish and leave to cool. To make the salad dressing, place the olive oil, lemon juice, coriander, salt and pepper in a bowl and whisk together.

Pour some of the dressing over the aubergines (eggplants). Halve the tomatoes and cut the labna into slices or cubes. Arrange the tomatoes and labna over the aubergine (eggplant) slices. Pour the remaining dressing over. Scatter the pine nuts on top and serve, garnished with sprigs of coriander.

Serves 4.

Variation: Feta makes a good alternative to the labna.

──BLACK-EYED BEAN SALAD──

350 g (12 oz) black-eyed beans, soaked overnight
salt
1 red onion, chopped
red pepper (capsicum) strips, to garnish
DRESSING
115 ml (4 fl oz/½ cup) olive oil
juice 1 lemon
1 clove garlic, crushed
4 tablespoons chopped fresh flat leaf parsley
1 teaspoon cumin
½-1 teaspoon harissa (see page 46)

Drain the beans and place in a large saucepan. Cover with water and bring to the boil.

Boil briskly for 10 minutes then simmer, covered, for 20 minutes, or until tender. Add salt towards the end of the cooking time. Drain the beans and place in a large bowl. To make the dressing, place the oil, lemon juice, garlic, parsley, cumin and harissa in a bowl and whisk together. Pour the dressing over the warm beans.

Add the chopped onion and mix well. Leave until cold, then transfer to a serving dish. Serve the salad garnished with strips of red pepper (capsicum).

Serves 6.

Variation: Other beans, such as flageolet or red kidney beans may be used instead of, or combined with, black-eyed beans.

-TOMATO, OLIVE & CAPER SALAD-

175 g (6 oz/1¼ cups) pitted mixed olives
2 anchovy fillets
6 tablespoons olive oil
1 tablespoon lemon juice
2 tablespoons capers
2 tablespoons roughly chopped fresh coriander
1 clove garlic, crushed
450 g (1 lb) plum tomatoes
salt and freshly ground black pepper
grated lemon rind, to garnish

Place 115 g (4 oz/¾ cup) of the olives in a food processor or blender with the anchovies, 2 tablespoons of the olive oil and the lemon juice.

Process for a few seconds to a coarse dressing. Transfer the mixture to a bowl, add the capers, chopped coriander and garlic and set aside. Cut the tomatoes into rough chunks. In a frying pan (skillet), heat the remaining oil. Add the tomatoes and cook briefly until just beginning to soften.

Add the olive mixture and reserved olives and heat for 1 minute until warmed through. Season with salt and pepper, remembering the anchovies are salty. Garnish with with grated lemon rind and serve with salad leaves.

Serves 4.

—WATERMELON & FETA SALAD—

½ small watermelon or a wedge weighing
   about 800g (1⅓lb)
130g (4½oz) feta cheese
freshly ground black pepper
12 pitted black olives
2 tablespoons roughly chopped fresh mint
2 tablespoons olive oil
2 teaspoons lime juice

Cut the rind off the watermelon and cut the
melon into cubes, picking out and discarding the seeds.

Arrange the melon cubes on a serving dish.
Roughly crumble the feta cheese over the
melon. Sprinkle with freshly ground black
pepper. Arrange the olives on top.

Scatter the chopped mint over. Mix
together the olive oil and lime juice and
drizzle over the salad.

Serves 4.

Variations: Sliced radishes or pomegranate
seeds may be added to this traditional salad.

——TUNISIAN ORANGE SALAD——

6 small oranges
1 fennel bulb
1 red onion
1 tablespoon cumin seeds
1 teaspoon coarsely ground black pepper
1 tablespoon chopped fresh mint
6 tablespoons olive oil
fresh mint sprigs and black olives, to serve

Cut the peel off the oranges, removing all the pith. Thinly slice the oranges, catching any juice.

Cut the fennel in half and slice it thinly. Slice the onion thinly. Arrange the orange, fennel and onion slices in a dish, sprinkling each layer with cumin seeds, black pepper, mint and olive oil. Drizzle the reserved orange juice over.

Leave the salad to marinate in a cool place for 1-2 hours. Just before serving, scatter the salad with mint sprigs and black olives.

Serves 6.

Note: Leaving the salad to marinate for up to 2 hours allows the flavours to develop and the onion to soften. However, do not leave the salad for longer than this before serving.

—CASABLANCA FRUIT SALAD—

4 oranges
2 peaches
4 figs
2 pomegranates
1 tablespoon orange flower water
icing sugar

Carefully cut the skins off the oranges, removing any pith. Cut the oranges into segments by cutting down between the membranes with a sharp knife. Reserve any juice in a bowl. Place the orange segments in a serving dish.

Place the peaches in a bowl and cover with boiling water. Leave for 30 seconds, then plunge into cold water for 30 seconds. Peel off the skins. Carefully cut the peaches into wedge shaped slices down to the stone; add the peach slices to the oranges. Cut the figs, lengthways, into wedges and add to the prepared fruit.

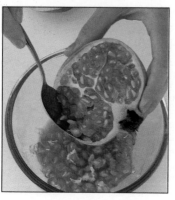

Halve the pomegranates and scoop out the seeds. Place about two thirds of the seeds in a food processor and blend for 2-3 seconds to extract the juice. Strain through a nylon sieve into the bowl of reserved orange juice. Stir in the orange flower water and sugar, to taste, and pour over the fruit. Scatter the remaining pomegranate seeds over and serve.

Serves 4-6.

—STUFFED DATES & WALNUTS—

12 fresh dates
45 g (1½oz/½ cup) ground almonds
2 tablespoons very finely chopped pistachio nuts
2 tablespoons caster sugar
orange flower water
24 walnut halves
icing sugar, to decorate

With a sharp knife, make a slit down the length of each date and carefully remove the stone.

In a bowl, mix together the ground almonds, chopped pistachio nuts and caster sugar. Add enough orange flower water to make a smooth paste. Shape half of the paste into 12 nuggets the size of date stones and use to stuff the dates.

Use the remaining paste to sandwich the walnut halves together in pairs. Sift a little icing sugar over the stuffed dates and walnuts and serve with coffee.

Serves 4-6.

–PEACHES IN CINNAMON SYRUP–

55 g (2 oz/⅓ cup) blanched almonds
115 g (4 oz/¾ cup) shelled pistachio nuts
½ teaspoon ground cinnamon
25 g (1 oz) caster sugar
1 egg yolk
6 ripe but firm peaches, halved and stoned
Greek yogurt, to serve
CINNAMON SYRUP
3 tablespoons honey
2 cinnamon sticks
2 tablespoons rosewater

Coarsely chop the almonds and pistachio nuts in a food processor, then stir in the cinnamon and caster sugar.

Stir in the egg yolk and mix to a paste. Preheat the oven to 180C (350F/Gas 4). Spoon the mixture into the peach halves and arrange the fruit closely in a baking dish. To make the cinnamon syrup, place the honey in a saucepan with 300 ml (10 fl oz/1¼ cups) water. Heat gently to dissolve the honey.

Add the cinnamon sticks and boil for 5-6 minutes until slightly thickened. Add the rosewater and pour the syrup round the peaches. Bake for 15-20 minutes until the peaches are tender but not falling apart. Baste occasionally with the syrup. Serve with yogurt.

Serves 6.

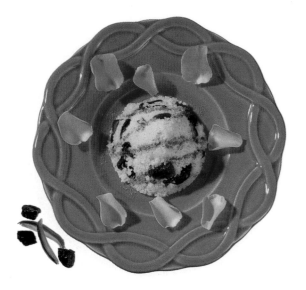

——SWEET DESSERT COUSCOUS——

250 g (9 oz) couscous
115 g (4 oz) fresh dates
115 g (4 oz) ready-to-eat prunes
85 g (3 oz) butter, melted
55 g (2 oz/¼ cup) caster sugar
1 teaspoon ground cinnamon
½ teaspoon ground nutmeg
rose petals, to decorate

Place the couscous in a bowl and cover with 150 ml (5 fl oz/⅔ cup) warm water. Leave for 15 minutes to swell.

Halve each date lengthways, remove the stone and cut into four. Roughly chop the prunes. Fluff up the grains of couscous with a fork then place in a couscoussière or in a muslin lined colander and steam over simmering water for 15 minutes until hot.

Transfer to a bowl, fluff up again with a fork. Add the melted butter, caster sugar, dates and prunes. Pile the couscous in a cone shape in a serving dish. Mix the cinnamon and nutmeg together and sprinkle in delicate trails over the couscous. Serve, decorated with rose petals.

Serves 4.

──ORANGE & ALMOND CAKE──

1 orange
115 g (4 oz/½ cup) softened butter
115 g (4 oz/½ cup) caster sugar
2 eggs, beaten
175 g (6 oz/1 cup) semolina
100 g (3½oz/1 cup) ground almonds
1½ teaspoons baking powder
4 oranges, peeled and sliced
115 g (4 oz) stoned dates, roughly chopped
icing sugar, to decorate
SYRUP
300 ml (10 fl oz/1¼ cups) orange juice
130 g (4½oz) caster sugar

Preheat the oven to 180C (350F/Gas 4). Butter and base line a 20 cm (8 in) cake tin.

Grate the rind from the orange, and squeeze the juice from one half. In a bowl, beat together the butter, orange rind and caster sugar until light and creamy. Gradually beat in the eggs. Mix together the semolina, ground almonds and baking powder and fold into the creamed mixture with the reserved orange juice. Spoon the mixture into the prepared tin and bake for 30-40 minutes until well risen and a skewer inserted into the centre comes out clean. Leave to cool in the tin for a few minutes.

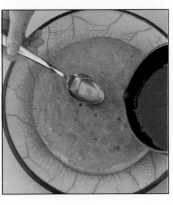

Meanwhile, make the syrup. Put the orange juice and sugar in a pan; heat gently until the sugar dissolves. Bring to the boil and simmer for 4 minutes until syrupy. Turn the cake out onto a deep serving dish. Using a skewer, make holes in the warm cake. Spoon three quarters of the syrup over, and leave for 30 minutes. Place the oranges and dates in the remaining syrup and leave to cool. Dust the cake with icing sugar and cut into slices. Serve with the fruit in syrup.

Serves 8.

– PISTACHIO & HAZELNUT ROLLS –

55 g (2 oz/½ cup) coarsely ground pistachio nuts
55 g (2 oz/½ cup) ground hazelnuts
55 g (2 oz/¼ cup) granulated sugar
1 tablespoon orange flower water
6 sheets filo pastry, 40x30 cm (16x12 in)
85 g (3 oz) unsalted butter, melted
icing sugar, to decorate

Preheat the oven to 180C (350F/Gas 4). Grease 2 baking sheets. In a bowl, mix together the ground pistachio nuts, ground hazelnuts, granulated sugar and orange flower water.

Cut each sheet of filo pastry across into four rectangles. Pile on top of each other and cover with a tea towel to prevent them drying out. Working with one filo rectangle at a time, brush the pastry with melted butter; spread a heaped teaspoonful of filling along the short end.

Fold the long sides in, slightly over the filling. Roll up from the filled end. Place on a prepared baking sheet with the seam underneath and brush with melted butter. Repeat with the remaining pastry and filling. Bake in the oven for 20 minutes or until crisp and lightly coloured. Transfer to wire racks to cool. Sift icing sugar over.

Makes 24.

—MARRAKESH SERPENT CAKE—

12 sheets filo pastry, 40x30cm (16x12in)
55g (2oz) unsalted butter, melted
icing sugar for dusting
ground cinnamon, to decorate
ALMOND FILLING
225g (8oz/2 cups) ground almonds
115g (4oz/¾ cup) icing sugar
grated rind of 1 orange
2 tablespoons orange juice
½ teaspoon almond essence
55g (2oz/¼ cup) softened butter

To make the filling, mix the almonds, sugar, orange rind and juice, almond essence and butter. Cover and chill for 30 minutes.

Preheat the oven to 180C (350F/Gas 4). Dust a work surface with icing sugar. Divide the almond paste into three and roll each piece into a rope 50cm (20in) long. Brush two sheets of filo pastry with melted butter and place side by side, with the long sides overlapping slightly. Place two more buttered sheets on top. Lay a roll of almond paste along one of the long sides and roll up. Place a hand at each end of the roll and press in gently so that the roll 'concertinas' very slightly. Brush with butter and roll into a tight coil. Place the coil on a baking sheet.

Make two more rolls in the same way. Join them to the coil, continuing the shape and sealing the joins with water. Bake for 20-30 minutes until crisp and golden. Invert onto another baking sheet and return to the oven for a further 10 minutes to brown and crisp the other side. Invert onto a serving dish and leave to cool. Thickly sieve icing sugar over the cake then sprinkle ground cinnamon from between finger and thumb in thin zig zags across the cake.

Serves 6-8.

–ARAB PANCAKES WITH HONEY–

450 g (1 lb/4 cups) strong white bread flour
6 g sachet easy-blend dried yeast
1 teaspoon caster sugar
1 egg, beaten
550 ml (20 fl oz/2½ cups) lukewarm water
vegetable oil for shallow frying
85 g (3 oz) clear honey
2 teaspoons orange flower water
butter and warm honey, to serve

Sift the flour into a large bowl and stir in
the dried yeast and caster sugar. Mix the egg
with half the water and gradually stir into
the flour.

Gradually stir in the remaining water, beat-
ing well until the batter is smooth and
creamy. Cover the bowl with a damp tea
towel and leave in a warm place for 1 hour
or until the batter rises and bubbles. When
the batter is ready, lightly oil a heavy based
frying pan (skillet). Heat the pan until it is
very hot, then reduce to a medium heat.
Drop 3 tablespoons of batter into the pan. It
should not spread out too much. Fry until
bubbles burst on the surface of the pancake
and it comes away easily from the pan.

Turn it over and cook the other side until
lightly browned. Place the cooked pancakes
in a heatproof dish in overlapping circles
and keep warm while cooking more pancakes. In a small saucepan, gently heat the
honey. Stir in the orange flower water.
Serve the pancakes with a knob of butter
and the warm honey.

Serves 4-6.

Variation: These pancakes are often served
layered with clotted cream.

FIG TARTS

350g (12oz) ready-made puff pastry
icing sugar for dusting
250g (9oz) marzipan
12 fresh figs
1 tablespoons clear honey

Preheat the oven to 200C (400F/Gas 6). On a floured surface, roll out the pastry to a thickness of 0.5cm (¼in).

Cut out 6 12.5cm (5in) pastry circles and place on a baking tray. Dust a work surface with icing sugar and roll out the marzipan to a rectangle 30x20cm (12x8in). Cut out 6 10cm (4in) circles and place one on each pastry circle.

Slice the figs thinly across and arrange overlapping slices on the marzipan circles (2 figs to each tart). Bake in the oven for 25 minutes or until the pastry is risen and golden. Brush the tops of the tarts with honey and serve, warm or cold.

Serves 6.

—————POMEGRANATE SORBET———

225 g (8 oz/1 cup) granulated sugar
4-6 large pomegranates
juice of 1 pink grapefruit
1 egg white
pomegranate seeds and mint sprigs, to decorate

Turn the freezer to its coldest setting. Put the sugar and 300 ml (10 fl oz/1¼ cups) water in a saucepan. Heat gently until the sugar has dissolved then bring to the boil and simmer for 5 minutes. Leave to cool.

Cut the pomegranates in half and squeeze on a lemon squeezer to yield 400 ml (14 fl oz/1¾ cups) juice. Strain the juice into the cooled syrup. Stir in the grapefruit juice. Pour into a freezerproof container. Place in the freezer. When the sides are beginning to set, transfer the mixture to a bowl and beat thoroughly, or process in the food processor or blender. Return to the container and freeze for 30-40 minutes.

When the sorbet is just beginning to solidify, whisk the egg white until stiff. Beat the sorbet mixture again until smooth. Fold in the egg white. Return to the freezer until firm. Transfer the sorbet to the refrigerator 20 minutes before serving. Serve, decorated with pomegranate seeds and mint sprigs.

Serves 4-6.

INDEX